Painting with Words

Michael &
Peter Benton

Hodder & Stoughton
A MEMBER OF THE HODDER HEADLINE GROUP

Poem acknowledgements
The authors and publishers would like to thank the following for their kind permission to reproduce copyright material: Tate Gallery Publications and the authors of the poems for the following from *With a Poet's Eye* (ed. Pat Adams): 'The Bowl of Milk' by John Loveday, 'The Lobster on the Telephone' by Eleanor Snow, 'The Badminton Game' by Connie Bensley, and from *Voices in the Gallery*: 'Giacometti's Dog' by Robert Wallace; Anna Adams for 'Boulogne Sands by P. Wilson Steer' and 'Totes Meer – by Paul Nash' from *Dear Vincent* (1986) published by Littlewood Press; Sylvia Kantaris for 'Gwen John's Cat'; Faber and Faber Ltd for Winter Landscape' by John Berryman from *Collected Poems 1937 – 1971* by John Berryman, and for 'The Uncertainty of the Poet' by Wendy Cope from *Serious Concerns*; Macmillan Ltd for 'Degas: Woman Combing' and 'Veneziano: the Annunciation' by R.S. Thomas from *Later Poems, 1972*; Seren Books for 'Father and Child: Ben Shahn' by R.S. Thomas from *Ingrowing Thoughts*; New Directions Publishing for 'The Great Figure' by William Carlos Williams from *Collected Earlier Poems*, and 'The Hunters in the Snow' by William Carlos Williams from *Pictures from Brueghel*; John Murray (Publishers) Ltd for 'The Highwayman' by Alfred Noyes; Rogers, Coleridge and White Ltd for 'Ophelia' by Adrian Henri from *Wish You Were Here*, published by Jonathan Cape Ltd, 1990 © Adrian Henri 1990; Valerie Bird for 'Looking Back' and 'Faux Pas'; Hannah Holland for 'The Paintbrush'; Heather Harvey for 'The Badminton Game'; Oxford University Press for 'The Balcony: after Manet' © Carole Satyamurti 1990, reprinted from *Changing the Subject* by Carole Satyamurti (1990) by permission of Oxford University Press; Anvil Press Poetry Ltd for 'The Virgin Punishing the Infant' by Carol Ann Duffy from *Selling Manhattan* by Carol Ann Duffy, published by Anvil Press Poetry Ltd, 1987; Orchard Books for 'Two Poems by Arcimboldo' by Julie O'Callaghan; 'Dancer' by Julie O'Callaghan copyright © 1983 by Julie O'Callaghan from *Edible Anecdotes*, reproduced by permission of Colin Smythe Ltd; 'Brueghel's Snow' © Anne Stevenson from *Four and a Half Dancing Men* by Anne Stevenson (1993) and 'I Would Like to be a Dot in a Painting by Miro' © Moniza Alvi from *The Country at My Shoulder* by Moniza Alvi (1993), both reprinted by permission of Oxford University Press; quotations which appear on p.43 are by courtesy of *Poetry Review*; 'Comic Strip', 'Waterfall', 'To My Daughter', 'Alice at 70', by Peter Benton and 'Suzon', 'In Limbo', 'Two's Company' by Michael Benton © authors' copyright.

Every effort has been made to trace and acknowledge ownership of copyright. The publishers will be glad to make suitable arrangements with any copyright holders whom they have been unable to contact.

British Library Cataloguing in Publication Data
ISBN 0 340 61873 6

First published 1995
Impression number 13 12 11 10 9 8 7 6 5 4 3
Year   1999

© Michael and Peter Benton 1995

Typeset by Selwood Systems, Midsomer Norton
Printed and bound in Great Britain for the educational publishing division of Hodder & Stoughton Ltd., a division of Hodder Headline plc, 338 Euston Road, London NW1 3BH by Colorcraft Ltd, Hong Kong.

Contents

CONTENTS

Painting acknowledgements
The authors and publishers would like to thank the following for their kind permission to reproduce material in this volume: The Tate Gallery, London for 'Boulogne Sands' by Philip Wilson Steer (p.7), 'The Bowl of Milk' (p.10) and 'The Bath' (p.11) by Pierre Bonnard © ADAGP/SPADEM, Paris and DACS, London 1995, 'King Cophetua and the Beggar Maid' by Edward Burne-Jones (p.22), 'Titania and Bottom' by Henry Fuseli (p.73), 'Lobster Telephone' by Salavador Dali © DEMART PRO ARTE BV/DACS 1995 (p.44), 'The Uncertainty of the Poet' by Giorgio de Chirico © DACS 1995 (p.40), 'Whaam!' by Roy Lichtenstein © Roy Lichtenstein/DACS 1995 (p.34), 'The Badminton Game' by David Inshaw (p.38), 'Totes Meer (Dead Sea)' by Paul Nash (p.46), 'Woman Holding a Black Cat' by Gwen John (p.55), 'Ophelia' by Sir John Everett Millais (p.68), 'Lady Macbeth Seizing the Daggers' by Henry Fuseli (p.53), 'Weeping Woman' by Pablo Picasso © DACS 1995 (p.85), 'The Great Day of His Wrath' by John Martin (p.88), 'Cossacks' by Wassily Kandinsky © ADAGP, Paris and DACS, London 1995 (cover detail) and p.89), 'The Toy Shop' by Peter Blake (p.90); The Tate Gallery Archive/The Paul Nash Trust for photographs of wrecked aircraft by Paul Nash (p.45); Réunion des Musées Nationaux for 'Spring', 'Autumn', 'Winter', by Giuseppe Arcimboldo (pp.14–15), 'Woman Combing Her Hair' by Edgar Degas (p.50), 'The Balcony' by Edouard Manet (p.60), 'Femme Cousant' by Mary Cassat (p.84), 'Le Berceau' by Berthe Morisot (p.87); Rheinisches Bildarchiv/Museum Ludwig Köln © SPADEM/ADAGP, Paris and DACS, London 1995 for 'The Blessed Virgin Chastises the Infant Jesus ...' by Max Ernst; The Fitzwilliam Museum, Cambridge for 'The Annunciation' by Domenico Veneziano (p.64); The British Museum for 'The Clod and the Pebble' (p.75), and 'The Poison Tree' (p.74) by William Blake; Phaidon Press, publisher of *Degas* by Keith Roberts, for 'Ballet Rehearsal' by Edgar Degas (permission unverified) (p.12); Photo Routhier – Document Archives Durand-Ruel for 'Dancer Tying Her Shoe Ribbon' by Edgar Degas (p.13); Bridgeman Art Library/City of Salford Museums and Art Gallery for 'A Fight' by L.S. Lowry (p.16); The Board of the Trustees of the National Museums & Art Galleries on Merseyside (Walker Art Gallery, Liverpool) for 'Customs House (North)' by Atkinson Grimshaw (p.17); Oxford University Press for illustrations from 'The Highwayman' by Charles Keeping (pp.18–22); Hessisches Landesmuseum for 'La Belle Dame Sans Merci' by John William Waterhouse (p.26); Sir Andrew Lloyd Webber Art Foundation for 'Oberon and Titania' by Richard Dadd (p.28); Bridgeman Art Library/City of Bristol Museum and Art Gallery for 'La Belle Dame Sans Merci' by Sir Frank Dicksee (p.24); Bethlem Hospital Archives and Museum for photograph of Richard Dadd (p.28); Louisiana Museum of Modern Art for 'Study for Cataract 1967' by Bridget Riley (p.32), and 'La Grenouille', 'La Tortue', 'Le Grand Assistant' by Max Ernst (p.80) © SPADEM/ADAGP, Paris and DACS, London 1995, photograph © Kjeld Kjeldsen; The Fogg Art Museum Harvard University Art Museums Gift of Prof. and Mrs. Josep Lluis Sert for 'Mural, March 20, 1961' by Joan Miró (p.42); The Museum of Modern Art, New York, gift of James Thrall Soby © Ben Shahn/DACS, London/VAGA, New York 1995 for 'Father and Child' by Ben Shahn (p.37); Alberto Giacometti-Foundation, Kunsthaus Zurich (Switzerland) © ADAGP, Paris and DACS, London 1995 for 'The Dog' by Alberto Giacometti (p.82); M.C. Escher Foundation for 'Waterfall' by M.C. Escher © 1994 M.C. Escher/Cordon Art–Baarn–Holland (All Rights Reserved) (p.33); The Metropolitan Museum of Modern Art, New York, Alfred Stieglitz Collection, 1949, Copyright © 1986/94 By The Metropolitan Museum of Modern Art for 'I Saw the Figure 5 in Gold' by Charles Demuth (p.36); Mauritshuis, The Hague inv. nr. 670 for 'Head of a Girl' by Johannes Vermeer (p.53); Courtauld Institute Galleries, London for 'A Bar at the Folies-Bergère' by Edouard Manet (p.60); Manchester City Art Galleries for 'Autumn Leaves' by Sir John Everett Millais (p.62), and 'Ophelia' (p.68); Kunsthistorisches Museum, Vienna for 'The Return of the Hunters' by Pieter Brueghel (p.76), and 'Summer' by Giuseppe Arcimboldo (p.14); Skoklosters slott, Sweden for 'The Librarian' by Giuseppe Arcimboldo (p.84).
Every effort has been made to trace and acknowledge ownership of copyright. The publishers will be glad to make suitable arrangements with any copyright holders whom they have been unable to contact.

Introduction

Painting With Words is a collection of paired paintings and poems suitable for work with secondary school pupils studying English, Art and related subjects. Most of the pairings involve a writer responding to a particular painting by making a poem about it; but there are also examples of painters who have illustrated scenes from plays or poems.

Our teaching approaches have two main aims:

- to indicate a way-in to the particular painting and poem which will engage pupils actively in careful viewing and reading;
- to encourage focussed discussion as well as creative and critical writing.

The material is arranged in three parts. The longest of these, *Seeing Things*, introduces pupils to the process of mapping their own responses to paintings and poems and to a range of activities which will help them to explore the two arts. The second part, *Perspectives*, is more demanding and includes more historical and technical information about the paintings. The third part, *Gallery*, is a small collection of paintings which can be used with any group for discussion and writing along the lines we have suggested elsewhere in the book.

Our experience suggests that pupils often find it easier to talk and write about paintings than about literary texts. Visual images are more readily shared: subject matter, colours, atmosphere, viewpoint are often more open to comment than is the case with poems. In many respects, painting is a more 'sociable' medium than poetry. One of the advantages of linking poems and paintings is that the latter can often provide a lead-in to a fuller and more confident discussion of poetry. The simple practice of making a sketch of a painting requires pupils to attend closely to its details and – labelled with notes about colours, shapes and so on – acts as a useful *aide-mémoire* when it comes to writing about the painting. A similar mapping of the readers' responses to the accompanying poem then offers pupils a unique encounter with the two arts working together in the imagination.

Finally, one particular issue that should be kept in mind is the nature of the image that the class is viewing. Reproductions are information, not art. They tell us *about* paintings but they can only hint at their materiality (see details, pp. 57–9 and 69–70). There is no substitute for the gallery visit to see the originals. This issue can be brought home in various ways:

- ask the class to examine a good colour reproduction of a painting carefully and to note what they see of the 'marked surface'. Can they see any paint, any brush strokes, any cracks – or just coloured dots? Although they may appear to give an idea of the texture of the original, it soon becomes clear that reproductions only show a flat pattern of colours and not the actual texture;

- as part of a gallery visit, ask pupils to make a close comparison of, say, a postcard of a painting with the actual painting, perhaps listing some of their findings on the back of the card;
- ask pupils to write down the sizes of the original paintings as they look at a varied selection of reproductions from books or in poster form. Then get them to visualise these actual sizes, maybe by discussing the best place in the school for these originals to hang.

Reproduced images are valuable as ways-in; they assume greater personal importance when they are reminders of original paintings seen in a gallery. Reading and discussing the poems that other viewers have composed about these paintings enriches the experience in ways that have the potential to last for many years. It is for this reason that we encourage the exploration of the visual and verbal together, both in book form here and through the resources of the art galleries (see pp. 95–6). We started with The Tate Gallery and our local art galleries – why don't you do the same?

Michael and Peter Benton

SEEING THINGS

When we look at a painting or read a poem, our attention moves from detail to detail as we build up our impressions. The thoughts that flit through our minds sometimes go so quickly that it's hard to capture them. One way of helping to focus our minds on what is before us is to make jottings about what we see or how we feel as we look at the painting or as we read the poem. Try this now for yourselves.

About a hundred years ago the British painter, Philip Wilson Steer, visited the French seaside town of Boulogne and painted this picture:

PHILIP WILSON STEER, *Boulogne Sands*, 1888–91, The Tate Gallery (London), oil on canvas, 61 × 76.5 cm

On your own

- Look carefully at the painting and jot down quickly what *you* see and feel. Do this *before* you look at our sketch where we have jotted down some of the thoughts that occurred to us as we looked at it.

In groups

- Share your ideas about the painting, describing to the others what you see. The thoughts that struck you might be different from the ones suggested on our sketch. Now turn to the sketch as you talk about the painting and discuss any new ideas it suggests.

Jotting down your own responses to a poem

In the same way as you jotted down your ideas about the painting, you can jot down your responses to a poem. Anna Adams, a modern writer, wrote this poem about the painting you have been looking at. Hear it read aloud first and then read it through again for yourself.

PHILIP WILSON STEER,
Boulogne Sands (detail)

— *Boulogne Sands* —

BY P. WILSON STEER, PAINTED CIRCA 1890

Each holiday, the sea's withdrawing room
became a brief Atlantis. Here, through art,
a coloured mirage shimmers in its frame.
Girls, disciplined by clothes – in light straw hats,
black stockings, muslin dresses – dig the sand
and build small tumuli. Bright bathing-tents
conceal their changing bodies, while the wind
whitens the dark blue waves that cunning paint
arrests and holds; so woven brushmarks fix
lost innocence on canvas, though high tide
chased all these children back to their hotels
a century ago. It scrubbed their works
from what proved to be minefields; here men died
where, long since, Granny built sand-citadels.

Anna Adams

Note down any ideas, pictures, or feelings that cross your mind. You will probably find some words and ideas a bit difficult at first. Don't be put off: somebody in the group may be able to help you – and you may be able to help somebody in the group. On the next page we have jotted down ideas around the poem: but we suggest you explore *your* ideas about it first before you look at our notes.

Talk about who you think these figures might be and what they are doing. Are any of them anything to do with the main group in the foreground?

Talk about who these people might be – their ages, relationships, what they are doing.

Do the way they are dressed, their hats and hairstyles, help you to place them?

Talk about what words you would choose to describe the mood of the group.

Talk about who is most involved, and who is least involved in the activity.

How does this figure help link the background of the painting to the group in the foreground?

Discuss what sort of atmosphere the *colours* and the *light* suggest to you. Think about the effect of the blue and orange against each other and of the splashes of white.

Imagine a photograph were taken of this scene. In what ways would the painting be different from the photograph?

Think about the way the paint has been put on the canvas (look at the detail of one part of the picture).

Atlantis was a fabulous island and city of great wealth and beauty supposed to have been swallowed by the sea in ancient times.

Discuss what this phrase suggests.

Tumuli are prehistoric burial mounds. Is this idea picked up later in the poem?

Talk about when there might have been minefields on this same beach. Who were the men who died here?

Boulogne Sands

Each holiday, the sea's withdrawing room
became a brief Atlantis. Here, through art,
a coloured mirage shimmers in its frame.
Girls disciplined by clothes – in light straw hats
black stockings, muslin dresses – dig the sand
and build small tumuli. Bright bathing-tents
conceal their changing bodies, while the wind
whitens the dark blue waves that cunning paint
arrests and holds; so woven brushmarks fix
lost innonence on canvas, though high tide
chased all these children back to their hotels
a century ago. It scrubbed their works
from what proved to be minefields; here men died
where, long since, Granny built sand-citadels.

Anna Adams

The modern word 'drawing-room' comes from the older word 'withdrawing-room' – a room to which the ladies would withdraw to chat together after dinner. Think about how the sea withdraws and who we see in the picture.

Talk about the way in which the painting is like a mirage. How 'real' is what we see?

Discuss what this phrase might suggest.

The skill of the painter captures the movement of the waves in paint and in the same way captures for ever the picture of innocent young girls on the beach – though they have now all grown old and died.

A citadel is a fortress defending a city.

Think about who is meant by Granny.

PIERRE BONNARD, *The Bowl of Milk*, c. 1919, The Tate Gallery (London), oil on canvas, 116 × 121 cm

— *The Bowl of Milk* —

In a moment the little black cat will be gone,
The bowl of milk set down somewhere
Outside the picture-space. Alone
Upstairs, Marthe will undress, prepare
The ritual water, soap herself, and lie
Becoming innocent. The cat will drop
Asleep in the sun, the milk bowl dry.
Bonnard will paint sunlight on the table top.

John Loveday

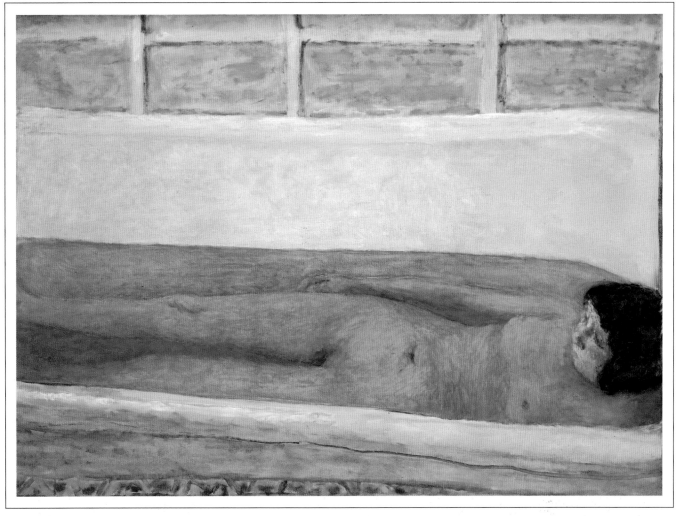

PIERRE BONNARD, *The Bath*, 1925, The Tate Gallery (London), oil on canvas, 86 × 120.6 cm

In pairs

- First, concentrate on the room in the painting (p. 10). Place a sheet of paper over the woman on the right and look at the room and balcony, noting all the details. What angle are you looking from?
- Now cover the room with the paper and look at the woman. What angle are you looking at her from? She fills this third of the painting. Notice her pose, her dress, and the effect of the light from the window: what impression do you have of her?
- Now, hear John Loveday's poem read aloud. Notice how the poem is in the future tense. Think about how the poem moves our attention, as it says, 'outside the picture-space'. How does this happen?
- Marthe, Bonnard's wife, was almost certainly the model for both paintings. Study the painting 'The Bath', above. Write your own poem to describe the feel of water, the sense of floating limbs, the colours and the geometric shapes of the bathroom.

EDGAR DEGAS, *Ballet Rehearsal*, 1878, Private Collection,
pastel and charcoal on paper, 49.5 × 32.23 cm

— *Dancer* —

I am a Degas dancer,
stopping before my performance
to fix my blue sash
and to wonder about dancing.

My shoe fits well,
I'm glad I'm here,
though sometimes I ache
and have to rest.

You won't be able
to see the ballet.
So judge me on how I stand
near the barre or tie my shoe.

If I do them well
then I am just as great
as the greatest
of all dancers.

Julie O'Callaghan

EDGAR DEGAS, *Dancer Tying her Shoe Ribbon*, 1886, Document Archives Durand-Ruel, pastel, 32 × 41 cm

Degas loved the world of ballet and captured in paint, pastel or bronze the figures of many dancers as they rehearsed, rested and performed. Many of his works are like quickly sketched 'snapshots' of people caught unawares. In fact, he did use a camera to capture many of the fleeting images, using the pictures as the basis for drawings and paintings done later, and with painstaking care, in his studio.

As a group

- Look carefully at the dancer standing adjusting her blue sash.
- What words would you use to describe her? How does she hold herself? What do you imagine she might be thinking?
- Now listen to the poem read aloud.
- Talk about what Julie O'Callaghan imagines is going through the dancer's mind. Is it like your ideas of what she is thinking?

In pairs

- Look now at the picture of the dancer tying her shoe ribbon.
- Quickly jot down and then discuss your ideas about the figure. Look for comparisons. What is the spread of her dress like? What is her hair like? The position of her foot?

On your own

- Write your own poem about the Degas drawing (p. 12). Try to capture what the dancer looks like and what she is thinking.

GIUSEPPE ARCIMBOLDO, *Spring, Summer, Autumn, Winter*, 1573, Musée National du Louvre (Paris), oil on canvas, 76 × 64 cm

— *Spring* —

She is a flower arrangement
hearing through a peony ear,
chewing with lily-of-the valley teeth.

Dew falls on her carnation cheek,
sparkles in violet eyes.
She talks with rosebud lips.

Julie O'Callaghan

In pairs

Make lists of all the plants, flowers and natural
details in each of these four paintings and say
which part of the body they represent. Arrange
your notes according to the season, like this:

Spring	*Summer*
lips – roses	eye-ball – cherry
shoulder of dress – cabbage	cheek – peach

Consider how the colours change from season
to season. Do you notice anything else about
how the heads change as the year progresses?

— *Winter* —

He looks out of a crack in the bark:
a white mushroom mouth,
a bare head of stubs, vines and roots

waiting for warmth.
The moss on his neck is dead
and yellow – an old stubble.

He is a grey ghost
hiding in the forest – warty nose
more pale than cauliflower ear.

Julie O'Callaghan

On your own

- Read Julie O'Callaghan's two poems and
  notice how she puts into words many of the
  items which make up the heads. Using your
  own lists, write the poems about 'Summer'
  and 'Autumn', in the same style.
- *Haiku sequence.* You may have come across
  haiku poems before. Haikus are three-line
  poems, or word pictures, which have
  seventeen syllables. There are five syllables
  in the first line, seven in the second and five
  in the third.
  On your own or with a partner, compose a
  series of four haiku poems, one for each
  season. ,

— Looking — Back

Only she looks back aghast to see the male delight in conflict.

A scene rehearsed, voyeurs egging on, boots, spit, and polish.

Should she stay to say 'enough, violence leads only to violence'?

Or will she walk away? The odds against her are ten to one.

Valerie Bird

L.S. LOWRY, *A Fight*, 1935, Salford Art Gallery, oil on canvas, 52 × 39.4 cm

In pairs

- Look at the painting and jot down some notes about:
  - the two men fighting, their positions and body language;
  - the onlookers, on the pavement, behind the railings, in the doorway;
  - the dogs and the setting.
- Now, hear the poem read aloud. Does it make you look at the painting differently?

On your own

- Using your notes, write your own poem from the point of view of one of the onlookers.

ATKINSON GRIMSHAW, *Liverpool Docks by Moonlight*, undated, Walker Art Gallery (Liverpool), oil on canvas, 60.8 × 91.2 cm

— *Faux Pas** —

Ships rigged on the left,
L'opéra to the right,
carriages splash through
an orange mist
the boulevard awash
with reflections.

Des magasins sont ouverts
pour saucisson, fromage,
ou des pâtisseries.
Mesdames et messieurs
se promènent sans parapluies,
late night shopping.

I peer at the plaque
beneath your painting
Atkinson Grimshaw,
not knowing your name,
to read my faux pas,
'Liverpool Docks by Moonlight'.

Valerie Bird

* French for 'false step' i.e. mistake

As a class

- Look at the painting and then hear the poem read aloud.
- What we see and what we are looking at are not always the same! Valerie Bird first sees this painting as a French impressionist picture, only to realise later that the setting is rather less romantic. What is it about the painting that produced this 'faux pas'?

Love, jealousy, betrayal, sexuality, violence, suicide, assassination, ghostly hauntings – all are here in Alfred Noyes's poem about Bess and her lover. The poem was written in 1913 and was illustrated by Charles Keeping in 1981.

As a class

- Hear the poem read aloud. The best way to do this is to accompany the reading with illustrations by Charles Keeping (*The Highwayman*, OUP, 1981) and to present these on an OHP: we have space for only a few small-scale illustrations from that book.

— *The Highwayman* —

The wind was a torrent of darkness among the gusty trees,
The moon was a ghostly galleon tossed upon cloudy seas.
The road was a ribbon of moonlight over the purple moor,
And the highwayman came riding –
　　Riding – riding –
The highwayman came riding, up to the old inn-door.

He'd a French cocked-hat on his forehead, a bunch of lace at his chin,
A coat of the claret velvet, and breeches of brown doe-skin.
They fitted with never a wrinkle. His boots were up to the thigh.
And he rode with a jewelled twinkle,
　　His pistol butts a-twinkle,
His rapier hilt a-twinkle, under the jewelled sky.

Over the cobbles he clattered and clashed in the dark inn-yard.
He tapped within his whip on the shutters, but all was locked and barred
He whistled a tune to the window, and who should be waiting there
But the landlord's black-eyed daughter,
　　Bess, the landlord's daughter,
Plaiting a dark red love-knot into her long black hair.

And dark in the dark old inn-yard a stable-wicket creaked
Where Tim the ostler listened. His face was white and peaked.
His eyes were hollows of madness, his hair like mouldy hay,
But he loved the landlord's daughter,
　　The landlord's red-lipped daughter.
Dumb as a dog he listened, and he heard the robber say –

'One kiss, my bonny sweetheart, I'm after a prize to-night,
But I shall be back with the yellow gold before the morning light;
Yet, if they press me sharply, and harry me through the day,
Then look for me by moonlight,
　　Watch for me by moonlight,
I'll come to thee by moonlight, though hell should bar the way.'

He rose upright in the stirrups. He scarce could reach her hand,
But she loosened her hair i' the casement. His face burnt like a brand
As the black cascade of perfume came tumbling over his breast;
And he kissed its waves in the moonlight,
    (Oh, sweet black waves in the moonlight!)
Then he tugged at his rein in the moonlight, and galloped away to the
    west.

He did not come in the dawning. He did not come at noon;
And out o' the tawny sunset, before the rise o' the moon,
When the road was a gipsy's ribbon, looping the purple moor,
A red-coat troop came marching –
    Marching – marching –
King George's men came marching, up to the old inn-door.

They said no word to the landlord. They drank his ale instead.
But they gagged his daughter, and bound her, to the foot of her narrow
    bed.
Two of them knelt at her casement, with muskets at their side!
There was death at every window;
    And hell at one dark window;
For Bess could see, through her casement, the road that he would ride.

They had tied her up to attention, with many a sniggering jest.
They had bound a musket beside her, with the muzzle beneath her breast!
'Now, keep good watch!' and they kissed her. She heard the dead man
    say –
Look for me by moonlight;
    Watch for me by moonlight;
I'll come to thee by moonlight, though hell should bar the way!

She twisted her hands behind her; but all the knots held good!
She writhed her hands till her fingers were wet with sweat or blood!
They stretched and strained in the darkness, and the hours crawled by
    like years,
Till, now, on the stroke of midnight,
    Cold, on the stroke of midnight,
The tip of one finger touched it! The trigger at least was hers!

The tip of one finger touched it. She strove no more for the rest.
Up, she stood up to attention, with the muzzle beneath her breast.
She would not risk their hearing; she would not strive again;
For the road lay bare in the moonlight;
    Blank and bare in the moonlight;
And the blood of her veins, in the moonlight, throbbed to her love's refrain.

Tlot-tlot; tlot-tlot!* Had they heard it? The horse-hoofs ringing clear;
Tlot-tlot; tlot-tlot, in the distance! Were they deaf that they did not hear?
Down the ribbon of moonlight, over the brow of the hill,
The highwayman came riding,
    Riding, riding!
The red-coats looked to their priming! She stood up, straight and still.

*Imitates the sound of horses' hooves by clicking the tongue against the roof of the mouth

Tlot-tlot, in the frosty silence! Tlot-tlot, in the echoing night!
Nearer he came and nearer. Her face was like a light.
Her eyes grew wide for a moment; she drew one last deep breath,
Then her finger moved in the moonlight,
    Her musket shattered the moonlight,
Shattered her breast in the moonlight and warned him – with her death.

He turned. He spurred to the west; he did not know who stood
Bowed, with her head o'er the musket, drenched with her own red bloo<
Not till the dawn he heard it, and his face grew grey to hear
How Bess, the landlord's daughter,
    The landlord's black-eyed daughter,
Had watched for her love in the moonlight, and died in the darkness
    there.

Back, he spurred like a madman, shouting a curse to the sky,
With the white road smoking behind him and his rapier brandished hig<
Blood-red were his spurs i' the golden noon; wine-red was his velvet
    coat;
When they shot him down on the highway,
    Down like a dog on the highway,
And he lay in his blood on the highway, with the bunch of lace at his
    throat.

And still of a winter's night, they say, when the wind is in the trees,
When the moon is a ghostly galleon tossed upon cloudy seas,
When the road is a ribbon of moonlight over the purple moor,
A highwayman comes riding –
    Riding – riding –
A highwayman comes riding, up to the old inn-door.

Over the cobbles he clatters and clangs in the dark inn-yard.
And he taps with his whip on the shutters, but all is locked and barred.
He whistles a tune to the window, and who should be waiting there
But the landlord's black-eyed daughter,
    Bess, the landlord's daughter,
Plaiting a dark red love-knot into her long black hair.

Alfred Noy<

CHARLES KEEPING,
'The Highwayman' illustrations,
1981, Oxford University Press,
various sizes

In pairs

- When you have read the poem through, make sure you have understood the plot. Then, jot down one or two examples of the following:
  - phrases that are repeated;
  - lines where rhymes or other sound effects help to create the atmosphere;
  - places where the rhythm of the lines gives a sense of the action.
  Talk about the use of repetition, rhyme and rhythm in the poem and why you think that the writer has used them to tell this particular story.
- Now study the illustrations.
  - The last picture repeats the first picture. Why is this?
  - How are the characters in the story presented?

On your own

- Design a poster which captures your idea of the poem; alternatively, create your own illustration for one of the incidents in the story.

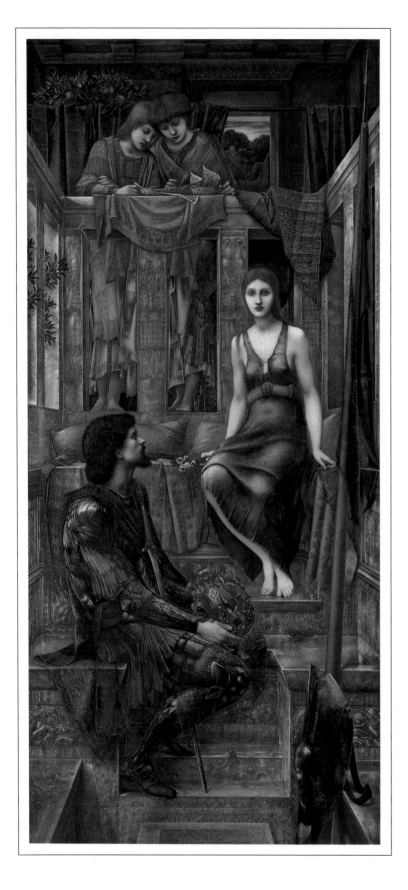

EDWARD BURNE-JONES, *King Cophetua and the Beggar Maid*, 1884,
The Tate Gallery (London), oil on canvas, 293.4 × 139.5 cm

Edward Burne-Jones knew the ancient legend of King Cophetua and the beggar maid from an old poem published in 1621 and a more recent poem written by Tennyson in 1853. So the poems inspired the painting.

King Cophetua was an African prince who cared nothing for women. Then, one day, he was looking from his window when he saw among the beggars at the gate a maid so beautiful that he fell instantly in love and had her brought into his palace. Tennyson continues the story:

— *The Beggar Maid* —

Her arms across her breast she laid;
She was more fair than words can say:
Bare-footed came the beggar maid
Before the king Cophetua.
In robe and crown the king stept down,
To meet and greet her on her way;
'It is no wonder,' said the lords,
'She is more beautiful than day.'

As shines the moon in clouded skies,
She in her poor attire was seen:
One praised her ankles, one her eyes,
One her dark hair and lovesome mien.
So sweet a face, such angel grace,
In all the land had never been:
Cophetua sware a royal oath:
'This beggar maid shall be my queen!'

Alfred, Lord Tennyson

In pairs

- Look carefully at the painting. In two columns jot down what strikes you most about the dress, appearance and expressions of the king and the beggar maid.
- Talk about why you think the artist chose to show the king in armour, with jewelled crown on his knee, his sword beside him and his lance and armoured breastplate leaning against the wall. In contrast, the beggar maid seems to be more simply dressed and carries only a bunch of anemones in her hand, some of which are scattered on the steps below.
- What is the effect of seating the king lower than the maid?
- Look at the structure, texture, colours and furnishing of the enclosure in which the king and the maid are seated. Why do you think this scene is set like this?

EDWARD BURNE-JONES, *King Cophetua and the Beggar Maid* (details)

In groups

- Share your ideas.
- Discuss how the story might have been written from the maid's point of view. An alternative version might have begun:

    His crown upon his knee he laid:
    He was . . .

  Can you continue a parallel version? Does she want him to be her king?

SIR FRANK DICKSEE, *La Belle Dame Sans Merci*, 1902, City of Bristol Museum and Art Gallery, oil on canvas, 13 × 18 cm

In pairs

Look carefully at the picture.
- What clues are there about the dress and appearance of these people to suggest who they might be?
- Where do you think they are?
- What is happening?
- Who is the stronger of the two and why do you think so?

As a group

Hear the poem read aloud. The title is in French and more or less translates as 'The Beautiful Lady Without Mercy', though perhaps 'without tenderness' would be more accurate.

- Look at the first three verses and talk about how the knight is described in the poem. What time of year is it? Where is he and what does he look like?
- Read on. What does the knight say the lady did to him?
- Which verse do you think best describes what you see in the painting?
- Describe the knight's dream and what happened when he woke.

Now look at Waterhouse's painting inspired by the same subject.

- What are the similarities and differences between the way the painters portray the two characters?
- Which painting do you prefer and why?

— *La Belle Dame Sans Merci* —

'O what can ail thee, knight-at-arms,
  Alone and palely loitering?
The sedge has withered from the lake,
  And no birds sing.

'O what can ail thee, knight-at-arms,
  So haggard and so woe-begone?
The squirrel's granary is full,
  And the harvest's done.

'I see a lily on thy brow
  With anguish moist and fever dew,
And on thy cheeks a fading rose
  Fast withereth too.'

I met a lady in the meads,
  Full beautiful – a faery's child,
Her hair was long, her foot was light,
  And her eyes were wild.

I made a garland for her head,
  And bracelets too, and fragrant zone,
She looked at me as she did love,
  And made sweet moan.

I set her on my pacing steed,
  And nothing else saw all day long,
For sidelong would she bend, and sing
  A faery's song.

She found me roots of relish sweet,
  And honey wild, and manna dew,
And sure in language strange she said –
  'I love thee true!'

She took me to her elfin grot*,
  And there she wept and sighed full sore,
And there I shut her wild, wild eyes
  With kisses four.

And there she lullèd me asleep,
  And there I dreamed – ah! woe betide!
The latest dream I ever dreamed
  On the cold hill's side.

I saw pale kings and princes too,
  Pale warriors, death-pale were they all;
They cried – 'La Belle Dame sans Merci
  Hath thee in thrall!'

I saw their starved lips in the gloam,
  With horrid warning gapèd wide,
And I awoke and found me here,
  On the cold hill's side.

And this is why I sojourn here,
  Alone and palely loitering,
Though the sedge is withered from the lake,
  And no birds sing.

*grotto or cave

John Keats

SIR FRANK DICKSEE, *La Belle Dame Sans Merci* (detail)

JOHN WILLIAM WATERHOUSE, *La Belle Dame Sans Merci*, 1893, Hessiches Landesmuseum (Darmstadt), oil on canvas, 112 × 81 cm

Shakespeare's play, *A Midsummer Night's Dream*, was written about 1595 as an entertainment at the marriage of a great nobleman; it was later performed in the public theatre. It has many kinds of amusement – songs, dances, a play within a play – and some beautiful poetry.

The plot brings together three main groups of characters: the young lovers, the ordinary working men (the 'mechanicals') and the fairies, led by Oberon and Titania. Theseus and Hippolyta, the rulers of Athens (where the action takes place), appear only at the beginning and the end of the play. They represent order and permanence in a play where the real world changes into a 'dream world' of the magic and madness of young love.

At the start of the final act, Theseus analyses the events that have occurred and speaks of the strange imaginations of lovers, lunatics and poets.

As a class

Hear Theseus's speech read aloud.

Lovers and madmen have such seething brains,*		* *i.e. boiling with ideas*
Such shaping fantasies*, that apprehend	5	* *wild imaginations*
More than cool reason ever comprehends.		
The lunatic, the lover, and the poet		
Are of imagination all compact.*		* *made up, composed*
One sees more devils than vast hell can hold;		
That is the madman. The lover, all as frantic,	10	
Sees Helen's beauty in a brow of Egypt.*		* *i.e. in the features of a gipsy*
The poet's eye, in a fine frenzy rolling,		
Doth glance from heaven to earth, from earth to heaven,		
And as imagination bodies forth		
The forms of things unknown,* the poet's pen	15	* *invents bodies for unknown*
Turns them to shapes, and gives to airy nothing		*things (e.g. fairies)*
A local habitation and a name.*		* *gives imaginary things a place*
Such tricks hath strong imagination		*and a name*
That, if it would but apprehend some joy,		
It comprehends some bringer of that joy.*	20	* *if the mind desires the idea of joy, then it*
Or in the night, imagining some fear,		*includes an imaginary person bringing it.*
How easy is a bush supposed a bear.*		* *similarly, the mind forms the idea of fear,*
		then creates fearful shapes.

William Shakespeare, A Midsummer Night's Dream, (Act 5, Sc. 1, lines 4–22)

- Make sure you understand what Theseus says that the madman, the lover and the poet each imagine (lines 9–17).
- Notice that lines 5 and 6 and lines 19 and 20 both speak of the mind's ability to 'apprehend' (i.e. to get a sense of something) and to 'comprehend' (i.e. to understand an idea). Talk about what you understand by these lines before hearing the whole speech again.

Nearly 300 years later, a painter whom the Victorians described as a madman produced a painting of Oberon and Titania. It shows the argument in Act 2 Scene 1 between the King and Queen of the fairies over the little Indian boy whom both claim as a follower. (You might want to look up the beginning of Act 2 in order to get the atmosphere of this fantasy world.)

RICHARD DADD, *Oberon and Titania*, 1854–8, Sir Andrew Lloyd Webber Art Foundation, oil on canvas, oval, 61 × 75.5 cm

In pairs

- Study the picture carefully. Notice how it is made up of minutely observed plants, flowers and trees, like still life painting, and also of many little incidents among miniature fairies and elves. Talk about these details and how they make up the overall design: some of the larger figures are taken from the play; many of the others are imaginary.

As a class

Richard Dadd worked on this picture for four years. The photograph shows him painting the tiny details into the outline plan. It was taken in the late 1850s amid the noise and violence of the criminal lunatic wing of Bethlem Hospital – or 'Bedlam'. Dadd had been committed there after he lapsed into violent and permanent insanity. The shocking incident that led to his imprisonment occurred when he invited his father to join him on a trip to Cobham in Kent. On the evening of their arrival, father and son went for a walk from which the father never returned. He was found later stabbed through the heart. Richard Dadd was eventually arrested for his father's murder.

- Look back at the painting. What gives it the sense of having been painted from a prisoner's 'seething brains' rather than directly from the natural world?

RICHARD DADD painting *Oberon and Titania*, photograph, 1857

The second painting by Henry Fuseli illustrates the beginning of Act 4 Scene 1: Titania has fallen in love with Bottom the weaver, who has been bewitched by Puck so that he has the head of an ass.

As a class

- First, read through the opening of the scene on page 30.
  How does the language that Shakespeare gives to Titania and Bottom suggest their characters?
- Now, study Fuseli's painting on p. 31.
  - How are Titania and Bottom presented to us here?
  - See if you can pick out the fairies. Look back at Shakespeare's text to see where to find them (Peaseblossom, line 6; Cobweb, line 9; Mustardseed, line 18).
  - The rest of the figures are creatures of Fuseli's imagination; some gaze at Titania, others stare out of the picture towards us. What is the atmosphere they help to create?

[*Enter Titania and Bottom, with the fairies attending, and Oberon behind, unseen*]

TITANIA:	Come, sit thee down upon this flowery bed,		
	While I thy amiable cheeks do coy,*		* *stroke*
	And stick* musk-roses in thy sleek smooth head,		* *fix, place*
	And kiss thy fair large ears, my gentle joy.		
BOTTOM:	Where's Peaseblossom?	5	
PEASEBLOSSOM:	Ready.		
BOTTOM:	Scratch my head, Peaseblossom. Where's Monsieur Cobweb?		
COBWEB:	Ready.		
BOTTOM:	Monsieur Cobweb, good monsieur, get you your weapons in your hand, and kill me a red-hipped bumble-bee on the top of a thistle; and good monsieur, bring me the honey-bag. Do not fret* yourself too much in the action, monsieur; and good monsieur, have a care the honey-bag break not; I would be loth to have you overflown* with a honey-bag, signior. Where's Monsieur Mustardseed?	10 15	 * *worry; also wear out* * *flooded by*
MUSTARDSEED:	Ready.		
BOTTOM:	Give me your neaf,* Monsieur Mustardseed. Pray you, leave your curtsy,* good monsieur.	 20	* *fist (i.e. shake hands)* * *stop bowing*
MUSTARDSEED:	What's your will?		
BOTTOM:	Nothing, good monsieur, but to help Cavalery* Cobweb to scratch. I must to the barber's, monsieur, for methinks I am marvellous hairy about the face. And I am such a tender ass, if my hair do but tickle me, I must scratch.	 25	* *cavalier (i.e. knight/nobleman)*
TITANIA:	What, wilt thou hear some music, my sweet love?		
BOTTOM:	I have a reasonable good ear in music. Let's have the tongs and the bones.*		 * *rough musical instruments used in the country*
TITANIA:	Or say, sweet love, what thou desir'st to eat.	30	
BOTTOM:	Truly, a peck of provender; I could munch your good dry oats. Methinks I have a great desire to a bottle* of hay: good hay, sweet hay, hath no fellow.*		 * *bundle* * *equal*
TITANIA:	I have a venturous fairy, that shall seek The squirrel's hoard,* and fetch thee thence new nuts.	 35	 * *store*
BOTTOM:	I had rather have a handful or two of dried peas. But I pray you, let none of your people stir me; I have an exposition* of sleep come upon me.		 * *disposition, desire*
TITANIA:	Sleep thou, and I will wind thee in my arms. Fairies, be gone, and be all ways away.*	40	 * *go away in all directions*

[*Exeunt Fairies*]

William Shakespeare, A Midsummer Night's Dream (Act 4, Sc. 1)

HENRY FUSELI, *Titania and Bottom*, 1780–90, The Tate Gallery (London), oil on canvas, 216 × 275.6 cm

- Finally, here is a modern poem on the same theme. Hear it read aloud and talk about how Titania thinks of herself, Oberon and Bottom.

— *Titania to Bottom* —

(FOR ALISTAIR AND BECKY)

You had all the best lines. I
Was the butt, too immortal
To be taken seriously. I don't grudge you
That understated donkey dignity.
It belongs to your condition. Only,
Privately, you should know my passion
Wasn't the hallucination they imagined,
Meddling king and sniggering fairy.

You, Bottom, are what I love. That nose,
Supple, aware; that muzzle, planted out
With stiff, scratchable hairs; those ears,
Lofty as bulrushes, smelling of hay harvest,

Twitching to each subtle electric
Flutter of the brain! Oberon's loving
Was like eating myself – appropriate,
Tasteless, rather debilitating.

But holding you I held the whole
Perishable world, rainfall and nightjar,
Tides, excrement, dandelions, the first foot,
The last pint, high blood pressure, accident, prose.

The sad mechanical drone of enchantment
Finished my dream. I knew what was proper,
Reverted to fairyland's style.

But Bottom, Bottom,
How I shook to the shuffle of your mortal heart.

U.A. Fanthorpe

BRIDGET RILEY, *Study for Cataract*, 1967, Louisiana Museum of
Modern Art (Denmark), poster paint and pencil on paper, 78 × 76 cm

— From a Picture by — *Bridget Riley*

To a surgeon,
Brain patterns.

To a junkie,
Hallucinations.

To a pilot,
Radar patterns.

To a physicist,
Waves.

To a child,
The sea.

To me,
Long hair.

Nick Dunning

On your own

- Look steadily at the picture for ten seconds. What happens? What do
  you see? What is it *like?*
- Quickly jot down any comparisons the painting suggests to you or any
  feelings it causes: *'It's like . . .'* What?

In groups

- Read Nick Dunning's poem which he wrote when he was thirteen. Six
  of you could read the poem, a 'verse' each (or three of you, each taking
  two verses). Were your comparisons similar or different?

On your own

- *Either* write your own poem in response to the painting, basing it on
  the ideas you jotted down at first, *or* continue Nick Dunning's poem,
  using the same pattern.
  If you continue the poem using the same pattern, you may find you
  can produce a longer poem by linking together the best ideas from
  your group or from the whole class.

— *Waterfall* —

'The miller simply needs to add a bucketful of water from time to time, in order to compensate for loss through evaporation.' (M.C. ESCHER)

Just looking at it makes me sick:
Nobody likes a clever Dick.
How it works I have no notion:
Just looking at it makes me sick,
Driven by perpetual motion.
Impossible! – a cunning trick!
Just looking at it makes me sick.
Nobody likes a clever Dick.

Peter Benton

M.C. ESCHER, *Waterfall*, 1961, Escher Foundation, Haags Gemeentemuseum, (The Hague), lithograph, 38 × 30 cm

In pairs

- Concentrate on Escher's drawing of the waterfall. Follow the flow of water from beginning to end.
- What happens? How is it done?

In groups

- Prepare a reading of the poem using eight voices, each voice reading one line. If you prefer, you could work in groups of four and take two lines each.
- When you have practised your reading, you may find you can produce an even more complicated effect by reading the poem as a 'round'. To do this, you will need to 'overlap' the voices, saying each line so that in the end all eight lines are being said at the same time.

On your own

Technically, this poem is in the form of a 'triolet'. A triolet is a verse of eight lines which has two rhymes. The first line is repeated as the fourth and seventh lines; the second line is repeated as the eighth.

- Write your own triolet based on this picture or on the equally disturbing op-art painting by Bridget Riley opposite.

Escher made many similar pictures and they are often reproduced as posters. If you can find another one that appeals to you, use that as the starting point of your poem.

Roy Lichtenstein, the American Pop artist, often based his paintings on strip cartoons. This painting uses the comic strip idea on a vast scale: it is actually over thirteen feet long and five and half feet deep!

ROY LICHTENSTEIN, *Whaam!*, 1963, The Tate Gallery (London), acrylic on canvas, 172.7 × 406.4 cm

— *Comic Strip* —

Comic Strip: The Art of War   by Lance Trueman

WHAAM!	**ZOW!**	**VOOM!**	I PRESSED THE FIRE CONTROL... AND AHEAD OF ME ROCKETS BLAZED THROUGH THE SKY ...
AND THE FUSELAGE ERUPTED IN A SHOWER OF FRAGMENTS. THE STARBOARD WING CRUMPLED IN A FLOWER OF FLAME.	TOO CLOSE FOR COMFORT THE GAPING SHARK'S MOUTH OF HIS ENGINE INTAKE LOOMED; THE FIREBALL SLAMMED THE CANOPY.	FOR A SPLIT SECOND I SAW HIS TERRIFIED WHITE FACE, FLESH PEELING BACK FROM OFF THE BONE.	**WHAAM!**  ... SHEER BLOODY POETRY.

PETER BENTON

In pairs

- List everything in the painting that tells you it is based on a strip cartoon.
- How do you respond to the painting? Is it serious? A joke?
- Is it any less 'art' for being based on a strip cartoon from a war comic?

Comic Strip was written in response to Lichtenstein's painting and tries to use similar techniques to those of the strip cartoon, but using words rather than paint. As Lichtenstein's painting plays mainly with the visual elements we associate with comic strips to produce a kind of grim humour, so this 'poem' plays with the kinds of *words* associated with such strips. It uses puns – words with double meanings – quite a lot. Some are even hidden in the small print.

- Does the poem have a message? *Is* it a poem?

On your own

Write your own strip cartoon poem based on a few frames of a romantic photo-story in a teen magazine, frames from *Batman* comics, football comics, or even your younger brother's or sister's *Jack and Jill* comic.

William Carlos Williams remembers an exciting moment when he saw a fire engine dashing through dark city streets.

CHARLES DEMUTH, *I Saw the Figure 5 in Gold*, 1928, Metropolitan Museum of Art, Alfred Steiglitz Collection, oil on composition board, 91.4 × 75.61 cm

— *The Great Figure* —

Among the rain
and lights
I saw the figure 5
in gold
on a red
firetruck
moving
tense
unheeded
to gong clangs
siren howls
and wheels rumbling
through the dark city.

William Carlos Williams

In pairs

- How many fragments of William Carlos Williams's name can you find in the painting?
- What is the mood of the painting? Think about the main colours used, the lines and angles, the light cast by the lamps. What is the effect of repeating and enlarging the number until it fills almost the whole space

On your own

- Do any numbers have a particularly strong significance or appeal to you? For example the number on the back of a footballer's shirt; the number of the house you live, or lived, in; a 'lucky' number; the number on the front of the bus that takes you home ...
- Select a number that means something to you and write your own poem about it. You can base it on Williams's poem if you like. Establish:
  - where you saw it ('Among the rain', etc);
  - what the number is and its colour ('I saw the figure ... in ...');
  - what it does (e.g. movements, sounds, colours associated with it).
- Can you match your poem with an illustration of your own?

Refugees are as numerous today as when this picture was painted. Here, the family walks away from the town, the father carrying the future (their child), the mother carrying the past (the portrait of her mother). Look carefully at the painting and then read R.S. Thomas's poem.

— Father and Child: — Ben Shahn

Times change:
no longer the virgin
ample-lapped; the child fallen
in it from an adjacent heaven.

Heaven is far off, back
of the bombed town. The infant
is human, embraced dearly
like a human mistake.

The father presses, his face set,
towards a displaced future.
The mother has salvaged her mother's
portrait and carries it upside down.

R.S. Thomas

BEN SHAHN, *Father and Child*, 1946, The Museum of Modern Art, New York, tempera on composition board, 101.5 × 76.1 cm

On your own

- Jot down your own notes on each verse. Be sure to ask yourself:
  - Who is 'the child' that the poet is thinking of? (verse 1)
  - Why might 'the infant' be described as 'a human mistake'? (verse 2)
  - What 'displaced future' might this family expect? (verse 3)

As a class

- Share your ideas with others and see if you can agree on a single sentence which states the theme of the poem.

DAVID INSHAW, *The Badminton Game*, 1972–3, The Tate Gallery (London), oil on canvas, 152 × 184 cm

As a class

- Study the painting carefully and list the ideas you have about the setting, the badminton players, the time of day, and the way details like the trees and the clouds are painted.
- Now hear the two poems read aloud.

On your own or in small groups

- Re-read the poems to yourself. One tells a story, the other creates a strange, dream-like image of another planet. Make a few notes about what you like or dislike about each poem, and decide which you prefer. Share your ideas with the group.

— The Badminton Game —

That morning, I awoke and went down
just as I was, in my green slippers
to look at the hydrangea mariesii –
the only flower Clifton allows in the garden
for he must have his trees and shrubs.

Out I crept, my slippers darkening in the dew,
and hearing a movement behind me
I turned and found Ruth. She was carrying
the racquets: and so – smiling, not speaking –
we ran between the great bushes to the net,

and there we played (quietly, of course,
so that Uncle Edward might not hear)
until the breakfast gong recalled us.
We ran up the back stairs en déshabillé,
and down the front ones, decorous but tardy,

and kissed Uncle Edward: but I took care
to embrace him as he likes best, to forestall
reproof. Colour rose up behind his moustache
and his face worked silently, but then he vanished,
as usual, behind *The Times*.

Connie Bensley

— The Badminton Game —

This is a green planet.
    We can see Earth from here,
    Ringed with light in the clear air,
    Where wind-shattered clouds give way
    To the blue curve of open sky.

The evening slowly revolves.
    The shuttlecock drifts.
    Arms lift, and shadows stretch
    Down over the wide lawns.

The trees are here today.
    Inquisitive but wary,
    It took them three days to move
    Up from their long meadows,
    And round the corner of the house,
    As if on huge, invisible wheels.
    Now they watch us, leaning together
    Looking over each other's shoulders.

The day is ending.
    Beyond us high walls wrap themselves with leaves,
    The pale hydrangeas droop in sleep,
    And dusk flows over the cool hills.

This is a green planet,
We can see Earth from here.

Heather Harvey

The Italian artist, Giorgio de Chirico, painted a strange dreamlike world in which ancient images – (old buildings, statues) are fused with modern ones (steam trains, bananas). He aimed to produce what he described as 'a highly troubling dream reality'.

GIORGIO DE CHIRICO, *The Uncertainty of the Poet*, 1913, The Tate Gallery (London), oil on canvas, 106 × 94 cm

In pairs

- What do *you* make of de Chirico's 'dream reality'? Think about the images, the strange perspective, the light and the shadows. Does it remind you of any other images you may have seen?
- If you had to explain the picture to somebody else, what would you say?
- Share your ideas about the painting with the rest of the group.

As a group

In her poem, Wendy Cope tries to capture something of the strangeness of de Chirico's dream world. She also pokes a bit of light-hearted fun at it for, as a poet herself, de Chirico's title intrigued her.

Hannah Holland was a year 8 pupil when she wrote her poem, *The Paintbrush*, after looking at the painting and enjoying Wendy Cope's poem.

- Hear both poems read aloud.
- In groups, rehearse your own reading of one of the poems with different people taking different pairs of lines.

— The Uncertainty of the Poet —

I am a poet.
I am very fond of bananas.

I am bananas.
I am very fond of a poet.

I am a poet of bananas.
I am very fond,

A fond poet of 'I am, I am' –
Very bananas,

Fond of 'Am I bananas?
Am I?' – a very poet.

Bananas of a poet!
Am I fond? Am I very?

Poet bananas! I am.
I am fond of a 'very'.

I am of very fond bananas.
Am I a poet?

Wendy Cope

— The Paintbrush —

I am a painter.
I love my brush.

I am a brush,
I love my painter.

I brush my painter.
I, a love, am.

A painter I love,
My brush I am.

Painter, my love,
I am a brush.

Hannah Holland

On your own

- Write your own poem in response to the painting. You could use the form pioneered by Wendy Cope and Hannah, if you like. Stuck for a starting point? 'I am a banana' or 'I am a statue' or even 'I am uncertain' might get you going!

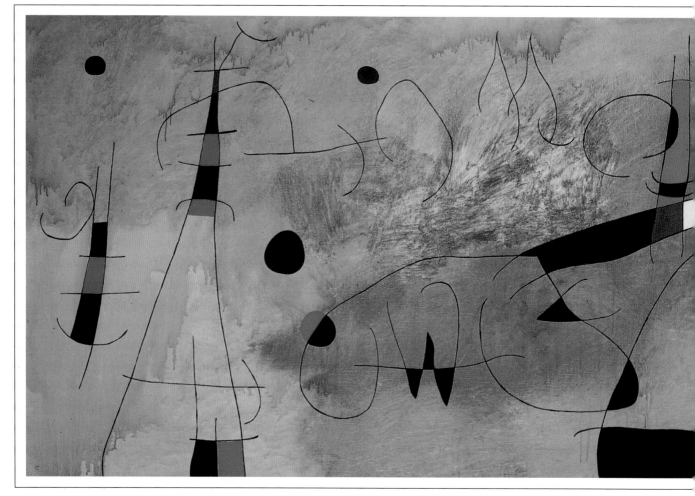

JOAN MIRO, *Mural, March 20, 1961*, 1961, Collection Josep Lluis Sert (USA), oil on canvas, 114.3 × 365.8 cm

— *I Would Like to be a Dot in a Painting by Miro* —

I would like to be a dot in a painting by Miro.

Barely distinguishable from other dots,
it's true, but quite uniquely placed.
And from my dark centre

I'd survey the beauty of the linescape
and wonder—would it be worthwhile
to roll myself towards the lemon stripe,

Centrally poised, and push my curves
against its edge, to get myself
a little extra attention?

But it's fine where I am.
I'll never make out what's going on
around me, and that's the joy of it.

The fact that I'm not a perfect circle
makes me more interesting in this world.
People will stare forever—

Even the most unemotional get excited.
So here I am, on the edge of animation,
a dream, a dance, a fantastic construction,

A child's adventure.
And nothing in this tawny sky
can get too close, or move too far away.

Moniza Alvi

As a class

Look at Miro's painting and talk about what the shapes and colours suggest to you. Now, hear Moniza Alvi's poem read aloud.

- The dot tells us quite a lot about itself. What sort of 'person' is it?

On your own

- Write your own brief comment – perhaps just one sentence – to sum up what the poem means to you.

Now, read and discuss the following reactions to the poem:

> I think Moniza is trying to get across the fact that not everyone is noticed. It's like judging a book by its cover. In the line 'People will stare forever', she means that finally she has become important. (Janine, aged 13)

> It seems the dot fancies the lemon stripe and it wants to be like the artist and survey the beauty of the linescape. (Tam, aged 13)

- Study the painting again and find *a detail* that appeals to you. Write your own poem, beginning: 'I would like to be a .... in a painting by Miro'

Insert your detail in this first line and carry on.

Salvador Dali was a surrealist who enjoyed creating dreamlike paintings where images were unexpectedly yoked together. Here an old-fashioned telephone receiver is taken over by, and almost transformed into, a lobster.

SALVADOR DALI, *Lobster Telephone*, 1936, The Tate Gallery (London), sculpture: mixed media, 18 × 33 × 18 cm

— *The Lobster on the* —
Telephone

I saw a lobster
Yellowish and orangish
Sitting on a telephone.
And I said
'Does your mummy know you are here,
You naughty lobster?
Did she say yes?'
The lobster curled his legs
Tiredly and crossly.

Eleanor Snow (aged 7)

In groups

- How does Dali mix dream and reality?
- Can you think of any other places where you have seen images that you would not normally connect, linked together in this surreal way? (e.g. record and CD sleeves, book jackets, advertisements, etc.)
- A pencil, a comb, a hairbrush, a calculator, a bag ... what creatures might these remind you of if you were thinking as a surrealist?

Write a poem of your own in which images are unexpectedly put together. The bag on the floor becomes a slug, perhaps; a hairbrush a ... well, *you* decide. Describe what you see. What, if anything, happens?

Paul Nash served as an official war artist attached to the Air Ministry during the Second World War from 1940–41. He based this painting on a set of photographs he took of a dump for wrecked German aircraft at Cowley near Oxford. The experience of visiting the dump affected him strongly and he wrote in a letter about the disturbing nightmare vision he had of this 'Dead Sea' of wrecked machines:

> The thing looked to me suddenly, like a great inundating sea. You might feel – under certain influences – a moonlight night, for instance – this is a vast tide moving across the fields, the breakers rearing up and crashing on the plain. And then, no: nothing moves, it is not water or even ice, it is something static and dead. It is metal piled up, wreckage. It is hundreds and hundreds of flying creatures which invaded these shores . . . . By moonlight, this waning moon, one could swear they began to move and twist and turn as they did in the air. A sort of rigor mortis? No, they are quite dead and still. The only moving creature is the white owl flying low over the bodies of other predatory creatures, raking the shadows for rats and voles.

PAUL NASH, *Totes Meer (Dead Sea)*, 1940–41, The Tate Gallery (London), oil on canvas, 101.6 × 152.4 cm

On your own

- Look at the painting and quickly jot down what you see. Make a list down the left hand side of your page. Like this:
    A waning moon low in the sky,
    Thin clouds,
  Try to list as many things as you can.
- When you have listed as many as you can, try to find comparisons for each of them to finish each line. Like this:
    A waning moon low in the sky, like a dirty snowball
    Thin clouds, like smoke
- Try to find comparisons that capture not just what you are *seeing* before you, but also what you are *feeling*.
- If you prefer, you can make a rough pencil sketch of the painting and jot down your ideas around the edge of it.
- Now look at the version of the painting on page 48 and think about the questions there. Some questions you may have asked yourselves already; some may prompt new thoughts.
- Finally, look back at Nash's original photographs and think about how he has used details and ideas from them in his painting.

As a group

- Share your ideas and comparisons.
- You may be able to develop your ideas and comparisons into a class poem with contributions from several people.

Listen to Anna Adams's poems read aloud.

—— *Totes Meer – by Paul Nash, 1940–41* ——

1

This picture is of waste. No victory
gloats in the absent eye that we make ours
by seeing what it saw. But tragedy
is not stressed either – we may keep our tears.

No beggar whimpers for them, we are shown
no scars, no mutilations, no burnt boys
but, bleached by moonlight, aircraft wreckage thrown
into an open grave for broken toys.

An Icarus has fallen from the sky.
Another and another fall, a rain
of torches must have fallen. This clear eye
records the waste, does not insist on pain.

Pity withheld is power; a reservoir
of weeping gathers, war-dammed in the brain.

2

The time is dawn. The moon
hangs on withdrawing dark
shedding just light enough
to cast shadows that mark
the sand. On ragged waves –
as rigid in arrest
as signpost dead – each crest
postures as though it lives,
threatens but cannot reach
with more than shadow-claws
the dead sea's desert beach:
yet this dry tide still gnaws
the fields away; lost land
submerges, all but drowned.

Anna Adams

It will help to hear the poems read more than once.

On your own

- Concentrating on each in turn, jot down any ideas, feelings, questions about the poems that come to mind. Is Anna Adams seeing the painting as you did when you talked about it?

As a class

- Share your ideas.
- Now look at the version on the opposite page, where we have jotted down some of the thoughts and questions that came to our minds as we read the poems. Some of these ideas you will have had already, others may prompt new thoughts.
- Anna Adams chooses a particular way of looking at the picture. Does it help the way *you* see it? Has her way of seeing it changed your view at all?

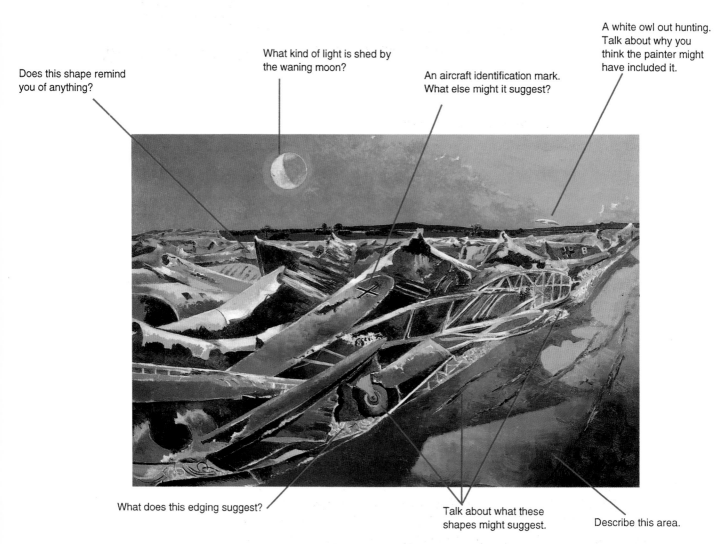

A white owl out hunting. Talk about why you think the painter might have included it.

What kind of light is shed by the waning moon?

An aircraft identification mark. What else might it suggest?

Does this shape remind you of anything?

What does this edging suggest?

Talk about what these shapes might suggest.

Describe this area.

Think about the colours and the light and the atmosphere they help to create.

Remind yourself what this means. Why do you think the British painter chose a German title?

Why do you think the poet mentions the date in her title?

— Totes Meer – by Paul Nash, 1940–41 —

1

Talk about the tone of these opening words and what has been wasted.

This picture is of waste. No victory
gloats in the absent eye that we make ours
by seeing what it saw. But tragedy
is not sressed either – we may keep our tears.

Talk about whose eye this is and how we make his eye our own.

If there is no victory and no tragedy, think about what emotions the poet feels the painting suggests.

There are no wounds, no bodies to see, no visible signs of suffering. What does the poet suggest the painter's feelings are?

No beggar whimpers for them, we are shown
no scars, no mutilations, no burnt boys
but, bleached by moonlight, aircraft wreckage thrown
into an open grave for broken toys.

An Icarus has fallen from the sky.
Another and another fall, a rain

Icarus was a young man who, in the ancient Greek legend, made wings of feathers and wax. He flew too close to the sun, which melted the wax, and he fell to his death.

Talk about how you see this in your mind's eye.

of torches must have fallen. This clear eye
records the waste, does not insist on pain.

Talk about what the word 'record' suggests. Remember that Nash was an official war artist.

Pity witheld is power; a reservoir
of weeping gathers, war-dammed in the brain.

The war had four more years to run. Talk about how holding back pity can be power.

What does this suggest about how the scene might be viewed in the future?

2

The time is dawn. The moon
hangs on withdrawing dark
shedding just light enough
to cast shadows that mark
the sand. On ragged waves –
as rigid in arrest
as signpost dead – each crest
postures as though it lives,
threatens but cannot reach
with more than shadow-claws
the dead sea's desert beach:
yet this dry tide still gnaws
the fields away; lost land
submerges, all but drowned.

Are these images – waves, signposts, threatening shadow-claws, a beach – similar to or different from your own first reading of the picture?

Anna Adams

- Consider what kind of poems these are. The first is a fourteen-line sonnet concerned with big, abstract ideas ('waste', 'tragedy', 'pity', 'pain'). The second is syllabic verse with six syllables to each line; it is much more a 'snapshot' in words of what the viewer sees. How do the first four or five words set the tone of each part?

EDGAR DEGAS, *Woman Combing Her Hair*, c. 1887–90, Musée National du Louvre (Paris), pastel, 82 × 57 cm

— *Degas: Woman Combing* —

So the hair, too,
    can be played?

She lets it down
    and combs a sonata

from it: brown cello
    of hair, with the arm

bowing. Painter,
    who with your quick

brush, gave us this silent
    music, there is nothing

that you left out.
    The blues and greens,

the abandoned snowfall
    of her shift, the light

on her soft flesh tell us
    from what score she performs.

R.S. Thomas

In pairs

Look at the picture of a woman carrying out the simple everyday task of combing her long hair. Clearly, given this subject, movement and colour are important.

- Talk about the *positions* of the woman's arms, hands and head. Do they remind you of anything?

As a class

Share your ideas about the picture and then hear the poem read aloud. One comparison runs through the whole poem. What is the key phrase? List all the words that keep the comparison going. Did any of the class see the same idea *before* you read the poem?

On your own

Perhaps other comparisons come to mind when you study the picture. If so, try to work these into a short poem of your own.

In pairs

- Look at the painting. This girl is looking over her shoulder at you across three hundred years.
- Talk about how she appears to you: how she is dressed; what she might be doing; what she might be feeling; the effect of the black background.
- Jot down your thoughts about her.

As a class

- Share your first impressions.
- Listen to the poem read aloud.
- Did your own first thoughts about the painting touch on the notions of fear and darkness or were they quite different, happier ideas?

— *To My Daughter* —

The identity of Vermeer's models is uncertain ... it is thought that this may be one of his daughters. Her turban may be part of the Turkish-style costumes, probably dressing-up clothes, which were among the effects left by Vermeer on his death.
(Marina Vaizey)

Dear girl, though three months past I've painted you
And patiently you've borne my old impatience,
You still have power to make me catch my breath.

A Turkish princess dressed in borrowed turban
You turn, lips parted, and with hare-eyed gaze,
Your face – by darkness called, by trust made bright.

So might Eurydice* have stood upon the threshold of the night.

Peter Benton

* Eurydice, wife of Orpheus in the ancient Greek legend, was called back to Hades when Orpheus broke his promise to the gods not to look back at her as he rescued her from the darkness of the underworld. As he reached the world of the living, he could not resist the temptation to look back at his beloved who, to his despair, vanished.

On your own

- Write your own poem about the painting, basing it on the jottings you made earlier. If you like, you can take the daughter's point of view and imagine what is going through her mind.

JOHANNES VERMEER, *Head of a Girl*, c. 1665, The Mauritshuis – The Hague, oil on canvas, 46 × 40 cm

The painter, Gwen John, lived in the Montparnasse district of Paris with her cat, whom she named Edgar Quinet after one of the streets there – the Boulevard Edgar Quinet. The cat appears several times in her pictures, often lying on the lap of one of the many women she painted.

In pairs

- Look carefully at the painting of the young woman. Talk about her dress, her appearance, her expression and manner.
- What is the atmosphere of the painting? Consider the colour and the light.

As a group

- Now hear Sylvia Kantaris's poem read aloud.
- What is the contrast between Gwen John's real behaviour ('forever waltzing out into the whirl of Montparnasse by night') and the world of the painting?
- Discuss why Sylvia Kantaris wishes Edgar Quinet had behaved as she imagines him doing.

— Gwen John's Cat —

I may never have anything to express except this desire for a more interior life.
(GWEN JOHN)

If you are a woman, try hard not to write about Gwen John. (ROSEMARY HILL)

Edgar Quinet (named after the boulevard
in Montparnasse) must have got fed up of
posing in so many glum girls' laps.
Dressed in slate-blues, greys or mauves,
they all fade into walls as if they had no choice.
Such a gloom of sitters came and sat and went
(woman in a necklace; woman with a jug, a book;
young woman holding black cat; herself).
I like to think that Edgar Quinet bristled,
scratched, brushed past and exited –
maybe came back with a *nature morte*
(a bird, a mouse, a dead leaf at least)
to liven up the canvases a bit.
If so, his gifts were fruitless.
Drawn into interiors as if to represent
the artist's lot (and she forever waltzing out
into the whirl of Montparnasse by night)
he looks as if he never could have settled
either this side of the door or that,
his eyes forever focused on an exit back.

Sylvia Kantaris

GWEN JOHN, *Young Woman Holding a Black Cat*, c. 1914–15, The Tate Gallery (London), oil on canvas, 46 × 30 cm

EDOUARD MANET, *A Bar at the Folies-Bergère*, 1881–82, The Courtauld Collection (London), oil on canvas, 96 × 130 cm

This painting shows the interior of the most fashionable *café-concert* (a kind of night-club) in Paris. Manet made some early sketches in the Folies-Bergère itself. The oil sketch and the final painting, both reproduced here, were painted in Manet's studio using Suzon, one of the barmaids, as the model.

On your own

- First, study the final painting. What do you see? Jot down some notes about: the main figures; where you, as the viewer, are looking from; the position of the bottles on the bar, and so on.
- Compare your ideas.

EDOUARD MANET, *Sketch for A Bar at the Folies-Bergère*, 1881, Stedelijk Museum, oil, 47 × 56 cm

As a class

- Now study the oil sketch.
- List the differences that you notice between the sketch and the final painting.
- Which of the two pictures shows the more logical relationship between the figures?

X-ray photographs of the final painting show that Manet made major changes while painting: the reflection of the barmaid was twice moved further to the right, and the position and appearance of the small, bowler-hatted customer were originally as in the oil sketch – he was only later replaced by the tall gentleman in the top-hat.

Now, hear the poem *Suzon* read aloud.

EDOUARD MANET, *A Bar at the Folies-Bergère* (detail)

— *Suzon* —

Behind my back I feel her slip away
Taking French leave; she edges so far right
Along the bar that I suspect Manet
Of wanting her discretely out of sight.
Our past is sketched: we make a faded pair
(Twice reconstructed since this all began);
The downward gaze, the fluffy piled up hair –
Perhaps we scared you, charliechaplin man!
Full frontal vacancy is now my pose,
My alter ego handles all the chat.
I long to perch a spy-glass on my nose,
Wear yellow gloves beneath a velvet hat;
But at my back I always hear her say:
'Now, Sir, what can I get for you today?'

Michael Benton

On your own

- Jot down your ideas about how the poem 'reads' the painting and its history. Try to comment on:
  - which lines refer to the oil sketch and which to the final painting;
  - who is speaking and what the speaker thinks of the other people in the pictures;
  - the form of the poem.

Discuss your ideas with others in your class or group.

EDOUARD MANET, *A Bar at the Folies-Bergère* (detail)

EDOUARD MANET, *A Bar at the Folies-Bergère* (detail)

Barmaids at the Folies-Bergère were both sellers and sold – mainly there
to sell drinks, but available themselves to the customers, at a price.
Suzon is placed between the 'real' bar with its richly-painted bottles,
flowers and fruit, and the 'unreal' world of pleasure reflected in the mirror
behind her.

- Read the second poem, *In Limbo*. Talk about the image of Suzon that
  the words suggest, the title, and the form of the poem.

— *In Limbo* —

Transfixed by your gaze,
Butterfly in a glass case,
Lost between two worlds.

Michael Benton

- Write your own haiku, or short poem, in response to the painting. You
  might focus upon one detail as a starting-point, for example:
  – the cut-off female legs and green shoes of the trapeze artist, top left;
  – the reflected customer at the bar, far right;
  – one of the minor characters watching the show.

EDOUARD MANET, *The Balcony*, 1868–69, Musée d'Orsay (Paris), oil on canvas, 169 × 125 cm

On your own

- Spend a few minutes looking closely at the painting.
- Jot down your feelings and ideas about what you see. Who might these people be? What are they doing? What do their dress, manner and surroundings suggest about them? What is the effect of the very formal framing of the picture by the green shutters and the neat triangles of the metal railing? Are there other formal triangles in the painting?
- Do you think there is a relationship between the figures or are they in their own separate worlds?
- What are the colours you notice most and what is their effect?

As a group

Share your ideas.
Now hear the poem read aloud.

— *The Balcony: after Manet* —

We form a perfect composition,
a triangle, he at the apex;
soft glutton's hands
smelling of sandalwood and Havanas.
Though I gaze down the street,
I know how his thumb and index finger
stroke each other, round and round,
oh, so slowly.
A woman's skin: a sheaf of banknotes.
I dig my fingers hard against my fan
to block the screaming.
I could gather up my skirts
and vault the rail;
or leap at him, plunge my nails
into those too easy going eyes.
But I sit here, tame as this agapanthus in a pot,
central, yet marginal.
My little sister with the holy look
falters on the threshold. Will she
step onto the balcony beside me,
her cachou breath warm on my cheek?
Or will she stay, give him
that second's sweet complicity
for which he waits,
a faint flush rising,
stroking, stroking?

Carole Satyamurti

Discuss how Carole Satyamurti reads the painting and how close her reading is to yours. Would a quite different reading be possible? Once you have discussed this, look at the note on page 93.

SIR JOHN EVERETT MILLAIS, *Autumn Leaves*, 1855–56, Manchester City Art Gallery, oil on canvas, 104 × 74 cm

In pairs

- Look carefully at the painting and, on your own, jot down what sort of atmosphere it suggests. Think about the effect of the evening light, the bare trees, the whisp of smoke from the burning leaves. Think too about the way each girl stands and about their expressions. Is this just a group of girls around an ordinary garden bonfire or is there something more?
- Discuss your ideas in pairs, then share them with the rest of the class.

Millais was only 26 when he painted *Autumn Leaves*. His young sisters-in-law, Alice and Sophie, were two of his models. Millais said he intended this to be a scene to arouse deep religious feeling. Many people see the girls' burning of the dead leaves as a symbol of the idea that, although everything dies, everything is continually renewed.

As a group

- Talk about how *you* read the picture.

Millais was a Christian and an optimist. By contrast, the writer of *Alice At 70* asks how Alice (on the left) might have thought about the painting when she was seventy.

- Listen to the poem being read aloud.
- What do you think? Do you see the painting as stressing the spiritual beauty of life and the idea of renewal, or do you identify with the bleaker and more pessimistic view expressed in *Alice At 70*?

— *Alice at 70* —

The two girls at the centre, one with a basket, one holding leaves, are Effie's (Millais's wife's) younger sisters, Alice and Sophie; the others are local youngsters, Matilda Proudfoot and Isabella Nicol, whom Effie had found to model. (MARINA VAIZEY)

I tried to look as John would have me –
Holding my basket *so* – and fixed my eyes on him,
Summoning a world of sadness to my wistful gaze
But, unlike Sophie, found it hard to keep my smiles in.
She loved the drama, holding centre stage –
A youthful priestess challenging our brother
As if to say when she consigned the papery leaves to burn,
'So it has always been, so it must be; I can no other,
All things that flourish are harvested in turn.'
And like a wingless angel, calm at evening prayer,
With downcast eyes, still Mattie clasps her broom;
Whilst little Bella, having bitten on the apple,
Ponders uncertainly what is yet to come.
Now, nearly sixty years on, she knows
That every tone and colour of our clothes and skin and hair
Is to be found within the tumbling leaves
And why those gaunt and twilit trees are standing there.

Peter Benton

DOMENICO VENEZIANO, *The Annunciation*, c. 1445, Fitzwilliam Museum (Cambridge), oil on panel, 28 × 54 cm

The title of this painting literally means 'the announcement' – it is the term used to describe the moment when the angel Gabriel tells the Virgin Mary that she is pregnant and will give birth to Jesus.

— *Veneziano: The Annunciation* —

> The messenger is winged
>   and the girl
> haloed a distance
>   between them
> and between them and us
> down the long path the door
> through which he has not
>   come
> on his lips what all women
>   desire to hear
> in his hand the flowers that
>   he has taken from her.

R.S. Thomas

MAX ERNST, *The Blessed Virgin Chastises the Infant Jesus Before Three Witnesses*, 1926, Museum Ludwig Köln, oil on canvas, 196 × 130 cm

In pairs

- Think about how Veneziano has chosen to construct this painting (p. 64):
  - First, concentrate upon the room. There are a lot of vertical and horizontal lines. How does the painter turn a flat canvas into a room and a pathway with such depth and spaciousness?
  - Secondly, study the two figures. Jot down some notes on their positioning in the room, their stances and the gestures of their hands to explain why you think they are presented in this way.
- Now read the poem through carefully. There is no punctuation to help you! Make sure you know where the pauses come and then practise reading the poem aloud.

- Talk about how the poem interprets the picture. What does the writer say about how we look at the room? How does he understand the flowers at the end?

On your own

- Write a paragraph to compare *your* reading of the painting with that in R.S. Thomas's poem.

As a class

In contrast to the traditional image of Mary and Jesus, the painting on page 65 presents a highly unusual view – Jesus getting a good thrashing and losing his halo!

- Study the painting and discuss:
  - how the two main figures are portrayed;
  - the feeling created by the three witnesses at the window.
- Now, hear Carol Ann Duffy's poem read aloud.

— *The Virgin Punishing the Infant* —

He spoke early. Not the goo goo goo of infancy,
but *I am God*. Joseph kept away, carving himself
a silent Pinocchio out in the workshed. He said
he was a simple man and hadn't dreamed of this.

She grew anxious in that second year, would stare
at stars saying *Gabriel, Gabriel*. Your guess.
The village gossiped in the sun. The child was solitary,
his wide and solemn eyes could fill your head.

After he walked, our normal children crawled. Our wives
were first resentful, then superior. Mary's child
would bring her sorrow . . . better far to have a son
who gurgled nonsense at your breast. *Googoo. Googoo.*

But I am God. We heard him through the window,
heard the smacks which made us peep. What we saw
was commonplace enough. But afterwards, we wondered
why the infant did not cry, why the Mother did.

Carol Ann Duffy

The poem explores this idea of the more human view of Jesus that is found in the painting.

- How do the villagers and the family react to having God among them?
- What do you make of the last sentence of the poem?

The death of Ophelia in Shakespeare's play *Hamlet* (Act 4, Sc. 7) was a favourite subject of Victorian painters. Ophelia was the forsaken love of Prince Hamlet. In her deranged state of mind, she decked herself with flowers and drowned in a stream. Read the Queen's description of what happened.

There is a willow* grows aslant a brook	* 'weeping willow' tree associated with forsaken love
That shows his hoar* leaves in the glassy stream;	* silvery grey
There with fantastic garlands did she come	
Of crow-flowers, nettles, daisies, and long purples	
That liberal* shepherds give a grosser* name,	* free-spoken * more vulgar
But our cold* maids do dead men's fingers call them.	* chaste
There, on the pendent boughs her coronet* weeds	* garland of wild flowers
Clambering to hang, an envious sliver* broke;	* spiteful small branch
When down her weedy trophies and herself	
Fell in the weeping brook. Her clothes spread wide,	
And, mermaid-like, awhile they bore her up;	
Which time she chanted snatches of old tunes,	
As one incapable* of her own distress,	* unaware
Or like a creature native* and indued	* belonging to and able to live in water
Unto that element. But long it could not be	
Till that* her garments, heavy with their drink,	* before
Pulled the poor wretch from her melodious lay*	* song
To muddy death.	

ARTHUR HUGHES, *Ophelia*, 1852, Manchester City Art Gallery, oil on canvas (arched top), 69 × 124 cm

SIR JOHN EVERETT MILLAIS, *Ophelia*, 1851–52, The Tate Gallery (London), oil on canvas, 76.2 × 111.8 cm

On your own

- The two painters have taken a different moment in Ophelia's death scene. Study the paintings carefully and jot down a few notes about the atmosphere and details of each.
- Write up your notes, comparing the paintings and saying which you prefer.
- Re-read Shakespeare's description. How do *you* visualise the scene?
- Sketch, paint, or make a collage of Ophelia's last moments or, if you prefer, describe what you see in your mind's eye in a piece of writing.

As a class

- Look again at Millais's painting. Simon Wilson tells the story of its composition:

Millais spent nearly four months from July to October 1851 painting the background, on the bank of the River Hogsmill at Ewell in Surrey .... In December Millais returned with the canvas to London, where he inserted the figure. The model was Elisabeth Siddal, who posed in a bath full of water kept warm by lamps underneath. The lamps once went out, she caught a severe cold and her father threatened Millais with legal action if he did not pay the doctor's bill.
The picture contains dozens of different plants and flowers painted with the most painstaking botanical fidelity and in some cases charged with symbolic significance. For example, the willow, the nettle growing within its branches and the daisies near Ophelia's right hand, are associated with forsaken love, pain and innocence respectively. The poppy is a symbol of death. (Simon Wilson, *Tate Gallery: an illustrated companion*, 1990, p. 83)

SIR JOHN EVERETT MILLAIS: *Ophelia* (details)

- Now, hear Adrian Henri's poem below read aloud. It is a poem about a love now gone and about the painting that the writer might have made of his own modern Ophelia, had their relationship lasted. Adrian Henri imagines the composition developing the other way round from Millais's: his Ophelia would start in the bathroom in Liverpool and only later would he add the natural details of 'a Devon riverbank'.

— *Ophelia* —

'There's rosemary, that's for remembrance:
pray you, love, remember...'

It is the painting I will not now paint for you.
Lying back in the upstairs bathroom
warm pink in a haze of warm water,
green with the essence of horse-chestnuts,
like the leaves hanging over her river.
1851, and in a golden summer
a man paints blue-flags*, dog-roses, a robin   * blue irises
perched on a twig. Nearby, his friend paints a cornfield
not yet occupied by lovers. A willow dreams
aslant a brook. Look deep into the green world
of pondweed. In winter he will paint her
dress enchanted with tiny ornaments in a bathtub
in London. In Liverpool you would have floated
breasts above the water, pubic hair tangled
like water-crowfoot. Later I would have painted you
a Devon riverbank alive with dragonflies, valerian.*   * a grassy plant
Viridian* depths. This is the painting I would have made for you   * green
my dark-haired, full-bodied Ophelia. But you are gone
and the image floats away downstream as shadows gather
in the green-carpeted bathroom. The lily-pads
of the bathmat you gave me remember.

Adrian Henri

- Re-read the poem and notice how it includes phrases from *Hamlet*, details from the painting, and evidence of the story of its composition.
- Write your own poem about one of the paintings – maybe including some phrases from Shakespeare's description, as Adrian Henri does.

Urged on by his powerful and ambitious wife, Macbeth, a general in King Duncan's army and Thane (Lord) of Glamis and of Cawdor, has murdered the king in order to seize the Scottish throne. He is so horrified by what he has just done that he forgets to leave the bloodstained daggers in the room with the king's drugged servants; this is what he and his wife had planned to do, to make it look as though the servants were guilty of the killing. Lady Macbeth sees that her husband is so full of guilt and remorse that he cannot re-enter the king's rooms, so she takes matters into her own hands.

MACBETH: Methought* I heard a voice cry 'Sleep no more;   * I thought
            Macbeth does murder sleep' – the innocent sleep,
            Sleep that knits up the ravell'd sleave* of care,   * a slender thread of silk
            The death of each day's life, sore labour's bath,
            Balm of hurt minds,* great nature's second course,   * cure for hurt minds
            Chief nourisher in life's feast.*   * nature's main way of feeding and
                                                   restoring us

LADY M.:   What do you mean?

MACBETH: Still it cried 'Sleep no more' to all the house;
            'Glamis hath murder'd sleep; and therefore Cawdor
            Shall sleep no more – Macbeth shall sleep no more.'

LADY M.:   Who was it that thus cried? Why worthy Thane,
            You do unbend your noble strength to think
            So brainsickly of things. Go get some water
            And wash this filthy witness* from your hand.   * evidence
            Why did you bring these daggers from the place?
            They must lie there. Go carry them, and smear
            The sleepy grooms* with blood.   * servants

MACBETH: I'll go no more:
            I am afraid to think what I have done;
            Look on't again I dare not.

LADY M.:   Infirm of purpose!*   * lacking in determination
            Give me the daggers. The sleeping and the dead
            Are but as pictures; 'tis the eye of childhood
            That fears a painted devil. If he do bleed,
            I'll gild* the faces of the grooms withal,*   * paint   * with it
            For it must seem their guilt.   [Exit]

                            William Shakespeare, Macbeth (Act 2, Sc. 2)

What picture do you get of each of the characters?

HENRY FUSELI, *Lady Macbeth Seizing the Daggers*, c. 1812, The Tate Gallery (London), oil on canvas, 101.6 × 127 cm

In pairs

- Look at Fuseli's painting. What do the stance and facial expression of each of the figures suggest about their state of mind? What do you notice about their eyes?
- What is it about their dress and the way their bodies are painted that suggests the terrible crime they have just committed?
- What are the main colours? Discuss why the painter chose to work with these.

On your own

This painting was inspired by Shakespeare's words. Nobody has written a poem about the painting. Jot down your ideas about the painting – everything you see and feel – as quickly as possible. Look first for comparisons: 'Eyes staring like . . .', 'Hands like . . .' and so on. From your notes see if you can write your own poem. (You might find it helpful to read the whole of Act 2, Scene 2 of *Macbeth* to put this extract into context.)

Blake was both a poet and an artist. He was not content to see his poems only as written texts. He thought of each poem-picture as an artistic whole and composed his illuminated books so that the two arts complemented each other.

These two examples, taken from his *Songs of Experience*, show Blake's typical use of trees and plants to frame his poems and his use of animals, birds, rivers and other natural details to symbolise ideas.

As a class

Read through the poems and study the paintings carefully.

WILLIAM BLAKE, *A Poison Tree*, c. 1790, The British Museum (London), coloured engraving, actual size

— *A Poison Tree* —

I was angry with my friend:
I told my wrath, my wrath did end.
I was angry with my foe:
I told it not, my wrath did grow.

And I watered it in fears,
Night & morning with my tears:
And I sunned it with smiles,
And with soft deceitful wiles.

And it grew both day and night,
Till it bore an apple bright.
And my foe beheld it shine,
And he knew that it was mine.

And into my garden stole,
When the night had veiled the pole;
In the morning glad I see,
My foe outstretched beneath the tree.

— *The Clod & the Pebble* —

Love seeketh not Itself to please,
Nor for itself hath any care;
But for another gives its ease,
And builds a Heaven in Hells despair.

So sang a little Clod of Clay,
Trodden with the cattles feet;
But a Pebble of the brook,
Warbled out these metres meet.

Love seeketh only Self to please,
To bind another to Its delight:
Joys in anothers loss of ease,
And builds a Hell in Heavens despite.

WILLIAM BLAKE, *The Clod & the Pebble*, c. 1790, The British
Museum (London), coloured engraving, actual size

In groups

- In *A Poison Tree*, the design is an illustration of the last verse. Talk about
  the argument and moral of the poem.
- In *The Clod & the Pebble*, the illustrations and the poem contrast
  innocence and experience. The innocent sheep drink from the river
  while beneath the poem the duck, frogs and worm prey on each other.
  How would you summarise what the soft, pliable Clay says about
  love in contrast to the views that the hard Pebble expresses?

PIETER BRUEGHEL, *The Return of the Hunters*, 1565, Kunsthistorisches Museum (Vienna), oil on wood panel, 117 × 162 cm

In pairs

- Look carefully at Brueghel's painting and list all the details you can see. Arrange your notes under three headings:
  - in the foreground (i.e. on the near hillside)
  - in the middle distance (i.e. the village and frozen lake)
  - in the distance (i.e. the fields, settlements and mountains)

As a class

- Share your notes and talk about the atmosphere of the painting.
- Read the first poem through to yourself; then, hear it read aloud. It's tricky, since there is no punctuation to help you.
- Which part of the picture does this writer concentrate upon?

— *The Hunters in the Snow* —

The over-all picture is winter
icy mountains
in the background the return

from the hunt it is toward evening
from the left
sturdy hunters lead in

their pack the inn-sign
hanging from a
broken hinge is a stag a crucifix

between his antlers the cold
inn yard is
deserted but for a huge bonfire

that flares wind-driven tended by
women who cluster
about it to the right beyond

the hill is a pattern of skaters
Brueghel the painter
concerned with it all has chosen

a winter-struck bush for his
foreground to
complete the picture

William Carlos Williams

PIETER BRUEGHEL, *The Return of the Hunters* (detail)

In pairs

- Now read John Berryman's poem and see if you can identify all the details he mentions. (Don't worry about the 'meaning' for the moment.) We can spot everything except the 'men with ladders' – have you seen them?

As a class

- Now hear the poem read aloud. You may need to hear it twice, for it is twenty-five lines and all one sentence! The subject and the main verb are far apart. Can you find them?
- The poem is written in syllabic verse – ten syllables per line allow the writer space to assemble plenty of details of this winter landscape. Notice how the details of the first two and the last two verses balance each other.
- Re-read verses 3 and 4 and say what you understand the main idea of the poem to be. Try to express it in your own single sentence.

— *Winter Landscape* —

The three men coming down the winter hill
In brown, with tall poles and a pack of hounds
At heel, through the arrangement of the trees,
Past the five figures at the burning straw,
Returning cold and silent to their town,

Returning to the drifted snow, the rink
Lively with children, to the older men,
The long companions they can never reach,
The blue light, men with ladders, by the church
The sledge and shadow in the twilit street,

Are not aware that in the sandy time
To come, the evil waste of history
Outstretched, they will be seen upon the brow
Of that same hill: when all their company
Will have been irrecoverably lost,

These men, this particular three in brown
Witnessed by birds will keep the scene and say
By their configuration with the trees,
The small bridge, the red houses and the fire,
What place, what time, what morning occasion

Sent them into the wood, a pack of hounds
At heel and tall poles upon their shoulders,
Thence to return as now we see them and
Ankle-deep in snow down the winter hill
Descend, while three birds watch and the fourth flies.

John Berryman

On your own

- Using your earlier notes about the details of the painting, write your own poem. You could shape your poem according to the three areas of the picture; alternatively, concentrate on one or two details that appeal to you.

- At the end of her poem, Anne Stevenson imagines herself in the world of the painting and wonders about: 'the unpainted picture'. She begins a poem about what happens next:
    'The hunters arrive, pull
    off their caked boots, curse the weather
    slump down over stoups ...'
Continue the poem.

— Brueghel's Snow —

Here in the snow:
three hunters with dogs and pikes
trekking over a hill,
into and out of those famous footprints—
famous and still.

What did they catch?
They have little to show
on their bowed backs.
Unlike the delicate skaters below,
these are grim; they look ill.

In the village, it's zero.
Bent shapes in black clouts,
raw faces aglow
in the firelight, burning the wind
for warmth, or their hunger's kill.

What happens next?
In the unpainted picture?
The hunters arrive, pull
off their caked boots, curse the weather
slump down over stoups ...

Who's painting them now?
What has survived to unbandage
my eyes as I trudge through this snow,
with my dog and stick,
four hundred winters ago?

Anne Stevenson

PIETER BRUEGHEL, *The Return of the Hunters* (detail)

MAX ERNST, *Three Bronzes*, 1967–74, Louisiana Museum of Modern Art (Denmark) Left: *La Grenouille*, bronze, 128 × 79 × 79 cm; Centre: *La Tortue*, bronze, 97 × 115 × 80 cm; Right: *Le Grand Assistant*, bronze 156 × 223 × 70 cm

As a class

Look carefully at each of these bronze figures: the photograph gives a good idea of their size and positions.

- Talk about how the two animals are portrayed – the frog stands upright, the tortoise has a smoothly rounded shape. What else do you notice about them? The third figure is more human: what do its expression and stance suggest?

In groups of three

Now read through the three-part poem. Clearly the figures are seen as a humorous trio of contrasting characters: the frog as a confident womaniser, the tortoise as a sultry female not to be easily won, and the onlooker as someone about to take drastic action. The three parts use different forms – playing on rhyming sounds, rhythmical variations and syllable patterns – to tell their story.

- Talk about how these forms help to create the three characters.
- Share out the three parts and rehearse a reading of the poem. Try to capture these three characters by your pace and expression. Present your reading to the rest of the class.

— *Two's Company* —

(In one of the gardens at the Louisiana Museum of Modern Art in Denmark there are three bronze sculptures by Max Ernst arranged as a triangular group.)

La Grenouille

He's a regular guy with a cool roving eye
Standing tall at an angle to passion,
Flips a few froggy quips from between his thin lips –
Woos her sideways after his fashion.
Yet he cannot disguise that hot look of surprise
As his eyes bubble out of their sockets;
He may seem so four-square, so laid back, debonair
With his hands plunged deep into his pockets;
But a heave of his chest intimates he's impressed
As obliquely he gives her the eye:
Should he leap at this chance like the bullfrogs of France
Or seduce La Tortue on the sly?

La Tortue

I feel as generous as French bread,
Firm as a silk cushion whose soft weight
The casual finger soon is tempted
To caress. Men but scratch my surface.
Shocking hairs curl symmetrically
Like the crown of some ecstatic palm
Shuddering, wind-tossed, down to its roots.
My pert head protrudes. Ambivalent –
I may just ease back inside my shell.

Le Grand Assistant

A spectator who clearly is outraged
    By this blatant attempt to seduce
Rises up like a heavyweight phoenix
   About to take off and lets loose
An indignant, censorious protest
    That both tightens the line of his lips
And should warn La Grenouille and La Tortue
    To avoid those bronze flaps when he flips.

His demeanour is so agitated
    His frame buckles, weak at the knees:
Does he threaten a quick levitation?
    Will he disappear over the trees?
Will he leap from his plinth in high dudgeon,
    Determined to stop this intrigue?
Or just crumple? – a clear indication
    That he suffers from metal fatigue.

Michael Benton

ALBERTO GIACOMETTI, *The Dog*, 1951, Alberto Giacometti Foundation (Kunsthaus, Zürich), bronze, 46 × 98.5 × 15 cm

— *Giacometti's Dog* —

lopes in bronze:
    scruffy,
        thin. In

the Museum of Modern Art
    head
        down, neck long as sadness

lowering to hanging ears
    (he's eyeless)
        that hear

nothing, and the sausage
    muzzle
        that leads him as

surely as eyes:
    he might
        be

dead, dried webs or clots of flesh
    and fur
        on the thin, long bones – but

isn't, obviously,
    is obviously
        traveling intent on his

own aim: legs
    lofting
        with a gaiety the dead aren't known

for. Going
    onward in one place,
        he doesn't so much ignore

as not recognize
    the well-
        dressed Sunday hun-

dreds who passing, pausing make
    his bronze
        road

move. Why
    do they come to admire
        him,

who wouldn't care for real dogs
    less raggy
        than he

is? It's his tragic
    insouciance
        bugs them? or is

it that art can make us
    cherish
        anything – this command

of shaping and abutting space –
    that makes us love
        even mutts,

even the world, having
    rocks
        and the wind for comrades?

It's not this starved hound,
    but Giacometti seeing
        him we see.

We'll stand in line all day
    to see one man
        love anything enough.

Robert Wallace

GALLERY

Browse through these pages as you might take a walk round an art gallery, pausing when something catches your interest. Find one or two paintings about which you can write your own poems. With either a postcard, photocopy, or your own sketch of the paintings, make up your own display on sugar paper. A collection of these displays from a group or class can make an effective wall presentation or scrapbook-style anthology.

GIUSEPPE ARCIMBOLDO, *The Librarian*, c. 1565, Skoklosters Slott, (Balsta, Sweden), oil on canvas, 97 × 71 cm

PABLO PICASSO, *Weeping Woman*, 1937, The Tate Gallery (London), oil on canvas, 60.8 × 50 cm

MARY CASSATT, *Femme Cousant*, c. 1880–82, Musée d'Orsay (Paris), oil on canvas, 92 × 63 cm

BERTHE MORISOT, *Le Berceau*, 1872, Musée d'Orsay (Paris), oil on canvas, 56 × 46 cm

JOHN MARTIN, *The Great Day of His Wrath*, 1851–3, The Tate Gallery (London), oil on canvas, 197 × 303 cm

* See note on p. 93.

WASSILY KANDINSKY, *Cossacks*, 1910–11, The Tate Gallery (London), oil on canvas, 94.6 × 130.2 cm

PETER BLAKE, *The Toy Shop*, 1962, The Tate Gallery (London), relief and various materials, 156.8 × 194 × 34 cm

$=$ *MAKING CONNECTIONS* $=$

Themes and projects

1 Making your own anthology

Either individually, in pairs or as a class, collect postcards of your favourite paintings. You will find lots of these on sale at art gallery and museum shops, at bookshops and at card and poster shops. Write your own poems to accompany them and present your anthology as a book or a wall display. If you use a word processor you can make your work look very professional.

2 Posters

Make a 'poster wall' in your classroom or along a stretch of corridor by displaying large-scale reproductions of paintings. First write to the main London galleries (addresses on pp. 95–6) to find out what is available. Explore your local galleries and bookshops too. Your school art department may be able to help. Don't forget other sources such as 'art' calendars which are are out of date within a year. The reproductions on these can be of very good quality. Gradually the class can build up a collection.

On your poster wall you might be able to feature a single artist one month and a group of artists another. You may want to explore other areas not covered in this book, for example African, Caribbean, Mexican, Indian or Japanese art. Whatever your choice, put brief notes about the artists, any information you can find about the painting and, of course, your own writing and poems in response to the pictures.

3 Tape/slide presentation

Put together a sequence of poems and paintings that you like as a tape/slide programme for a particular audience – maybe for pupils in another group, for an assembly or for children in a junior school. Think carefully about the theme or focus your programme will have. You can then write a script to link your paintings and poems and, of course, you can include some of your own poems too.

The easiest way of getting hold of slides is to buy them from the galleries at around 50p each, but you may also find that your school art department has a set and there are loan sets available from some public libraries.

4 Storytelling

Some say that every picture tells a story and it is true that every picture in this book has either a story embedded within it or one that could be invented about it. Choose a painting that appeals to you from here or from somewhere else and develop a story around it, either through discussion or through writing.

5 Gallery visit: making a *Student Guide*

Visit your nearest art gallery or one of the main city art galleries. Find two or three paintings that really appeal to you. Find out as much as you can about your choices. Buy a postcard or find a reproduction of the painting to help you remember the details.

Write a short account of your choices, including all the information you have discovered and the reasons why you like the paintings. If everyone in the group does this, you could put the pages together into a *Student Guide* for others to use. (Don't forget that galleries often have an education officer who will generally be only too happy to help you, particularly if given sufficient notice of your visit.)

6 'Desert island' paintings

Which six paintings would you choose to have with you on a desert island? Don't just confine yourself to our selection in this book; browse through other books such as those listed on p. 94, many of which will be available in libraries.

Compare lists and see if there are painters or paintings that are particularly popular.

If you could have just one painting on your island, which would it be? Write about the feelings and thoughts this painting gives you, either as a prose description or as a poem.

7 Men and Women

Several of the painting/poem combinations in this collection are concerned with images of men and women. As the great majority of the painters are male and often pre-twentieth century, they are likely to offer a male view of those images that reflects the attitudes of their own times.

Look back at: Tennyson's and Burne Jones's *King Cophetua* (p. 22); Keats's *La Belle Dame Sans Merci* and the accompanying paintings by Dicksee and Waterhouse (pp. 25–26); the portrayal of the relationships between Oberon and Titania and between Titania and Bottom which accompany the scene from *A Midsummer Night's Dream* (pp. 30–31); *Lady Macbeth Seizing the Daggers* (p. 73); Manet's *The Balcony* on p. 60 and his portrayal of Suzon and her customer at *A Bar at the Folies-Bergère* (p. 56); Keeping's illustrations for *The Highwayman* (pp. 18–21).

Look too at some of the individual images of women such as: the Degas dancers on pp. 12–13; Pierre Bonnard's paintings on pp. 10–11; women seen variously by Degas, Vermeer, Gwen John, and Millais on pp. 50, 53, 55, 68.

In groups

- Talk about the way men and women are portrayed in some of these paintings. Here are some questions to help you think about the topic:
  - Where men and women are shown together in these paintings, what rôle does each play?
  - Who is active and who is passive?
  - Who, if anybody, holds the power?
  - When women are depicted alone how are they represented?
  - Are there any similarities across the centuries in the way the painters have depicted male and female roles?
  - Do you think these same topics would have been treated differently by female painters?
  - Half the poems that accompany these paintings are by women of the twentieth century: do their poems reflect the same values and attitudes as those of the painters?

Note on Manet's The Balcony (p. 60)

Manet got the idea for this painting from a scene he first saw at the seaside resort of Boulogne-sur-Mer in 1868. The idea stayed with him, and he painted the scene later that year and in the spring of 1869 in his Paris studio, using friends as models. The seated woman is the painter Berthe Morisot (whose painting, *Le Berceau*, is on p. 87 of this book); the other woman is a young concert violinist called Fanny Claus, and the third, male, figure is another painter and friend of the family, Antoine Guillemet. The figure in the shadowy background carrying a jug is Leon Leenhoff, a boy whom Manet brought up. Does this information change the way you look at the painting or at the poem?

Note on Kandinsky's Cossacks (p. 89)

> … in the upper left portion of the picture are two horses rearing up against each other, their front legs interlocking. Each has a Cossack (Russian cavalry) rider wearing a tall fur hat which Kandinsky has here painted orange-red. Each is swinging a long curved sabre, painted mauve. Below the horses is a rainbow bridging a valley, and to the left of that, what appear to be two batteries of guns, one of which is firing, producing a cloud of red and orange flame. On the other side of the valley is a building suggesting a fortress and below it are three more Cossacks again distinguishable by their orange hats. Two of them carry long black lances and the third has his arm extended and is leaning on his sabre. A flock of birds flies agitatedly in the sky. (Simon Wilson, *Tate Gallery: an illustrated companion*, 1990, p. 143)

BOOKS TO TAKE YOU FURTHER

Apart from the first three titles in the General List, these selections focus on painting. Lists of poetry books can be found in our *Examining Poetry*, and there are extensive collections of poems in our *Poetry Workshop* and the five volumes of *Touchstones*. The second list is based solely on painters represented in this book.

General

Dannie and John Abse (eds)	*Voices in the Gallery*	The Tate Gallery
Pat Adams (ed.)	*With a Poet's Eye*	The Tate Gallery
Michael and Peter Benton (eds)	*Double Vision*	Hodder & Stoughton / The Tate Gallery
Michael Cassin	*More than meets the eye: a closer look at paintings in the National Gallery*	National Gallery
Robert Cumming	*Just Look*	Kestrel
Robert Cumming	*Just Imagine*	Kestrel
Marina Vaizey	*100 Masterpieces of Art*	Peerage Books
Piero Ventura	*Great Painters*	Kingfisher Books
Simon Wilson	*Tate Gallery: an illustrated companion*	The Tate Gallery
Susan Woodford	*Looking at Pictures*	C.U.P.

Individual painters and movements

—	*Arcimboldo Poster Book*	Taco, Berlin
Richard Kendall	*Degas By Himself*	Macdonald Orbis
Julian Spalding	*Lowry*	Phaidon
Jeremy Maas	*Victorian Painters*	Barrie & Jenkins
Christopher Wood	*The Pre-Raphaelites*	Weidenfeld & Nicolson
—	*The Graphic World of M.C. Escher*	Macdonald & Jane's
C. Langdale and D.F. Jenkins	*Gwen John: an interior life*	Phaidon
William Gaunt	*The Impressionists*	Thames & Hudson
Robert L. Herbert	*Impressionism*	Yale University Press
Sir Geoffrey Keynes (ed.)	*William Blake: Songs of Innocence & Experience*	O.U.P./Trianon Press
Gregory Martin	*Brueghel*	Bracken Books
Sophia Craze	*Mary Cassatt*	Magna Books
Alexander Robertson	*Atkinson Grimshaw*	Phaidon
Roland Penrose	*Picasso*	Phaidon

GALLERY INFORMATION

For a full list see *Museums and Galleries in Great Britain and Ireland* (ABC Historic Publications). Times of opening are Monday–Saturday (Sunday). For bank holidays and festivals, visitors are advised to check opening times in advance. STD codes given are from London.

Aberdeen
Art Gallery and Museums, Schoolhill. 10–5; Thu 10–8 (2–5). Tel: 0224 646333

Belfast
Ulster Museum, Botanic Gardens BT9 5AB. Mon–Fri 10–4.50; Sat 1–4.50 (2–4.50). Tel 0232 381251

Birmingham
City Museum and Art Gallery, Chamberlain Square B3 3DH. 9.30–5 (2–5). Tel: 021-235 2834
Barber Institute of Fine Arts. The University B15 2TS. Normally open to the public (parties by appointment only). 10–5; Sat 10–1, except when the Unversity is closed. Tel: 021-472 0962

Bristol
City of Bristol Museum and Art Gallery, Queen's Road BS8 1RL. 10–5 (closed Sundays). Tel: 0272 29971

Cambridge
Fitzwilliam Museum, Trumpington Street. Tues–Fri 10–5 (lower galleries 10–2; upper galleries 2–5); Sat 10–5 (2.15–5). For details contact the museum. Tel: 0223 332900

Cardiff
National Museum of Wales. Tues–Sat 10–5 (2.30–5). Closed Mondays. Tel: 0222 397951

Dublin
National Gallery of Ireland, Merrion Square, West 2. 10–6; Thu 10–9 (2–5). Tel: 0001 615133

Edinburgh
National Gallery of Scotland, The Mound EH2 2EL. 10–5 (2–5). Tel: 031-556 8921
Scottish National Gallery of Modern Art, Belford Road EH4 3DR. 10–5 (2–5). Tel: 031-556 8921
Scottish National Portrait Gallery, Queen Street EH2 1JD. 10–5 (2–5). Tel: 031-556 8921

Glasgow
Art Gallery and Museum, Kelvingrose. 10–5 (2–5). Tel: 041-357 3929
Burrel Collection, 2060 Pollokshaws Road G43 1AT. 10–5 (2–5). Tel: 041-649 7151
Hunterian Art Gallery, 82 Hillhead Street. Mon–Fri 9.30–5; Sat 9.30–1. Closed Sundays. Tel: 041-339 8855 ext. 7431
Pollok House, 2060 Pollokshaws Road. 10–5 (2–5). Tel: 041-632 0274

Hull
Ferens Art Gallery, Queen Victoria Square. 10–5 (1.30–4.30). Tel: 0482 222750

Leeds
City Art Gallery. Mon–Fri 10–6 (late night opening, Wed until 9pm); Sat 10–4 (2–5). Henry Moore Centre for the Study of Sculpture. Mon–Fri 10–1; 2–5 (or by appointment). Tel: 0532 462495

Liverpool
Walker Art Gallery, William Brown Street L3 8EL. 10–5 (2–5). Tel: 051-207 0001
Sudley Art Gallery, Mossley Hill Road. 10–5 (2–5). Tel: 051-724 3245
Lady Lever Art Gallery, Port Sunlight. 10–5 (2–5). Tel: 051-645 3623
Tate Gallery Liverpool, Albert Dock L3 4BB. Tues–Sat 11–7 (11–7). Closed Mondays. Tel: 051-709 3223

Manchester
City Art Gallery, Mosley Street. 10–6 (2–6). Tel: 061-236 9422
Whitworth Art Gallery, University of Manchester, Oxford Road. 10–5; Thu 10–9. Closed Sunday. Tel: 061-273 4865

Newcastle upon Tyne
Laing Art Gallery, Higham Place. Mon–Fri 10–5.30; Sat 10–4.30 (2.30–5.30). Tel: 0632 327734/326989

Oxford
Ashmolean Museum of Art and Archaeology. Tues–Sat 10–4 (2–4). Tel: 0865 278000

Sheffield
Graves Art Gallery, Surrey Street 1. 10–8.30 (2–5). Tel: 0742 734781
Mappin Art Gallery, Weston Park. 10–5 (2–5). Tel: 0742 726281/754091
Ruskin Gallery, 101 Norfolk Street. Mon–Fri 10–7.30; Sat 10–5. Closed Sundays. Tel: 0742 734781

Southampton
Art Gallery, Civic Centre. Tue–Fri 10–5; Thu 10–8; Sat 10–4 (2–5). Closed Mondays. Tel: 0703 223855 769
Swansea
Swansea Museum Service, Glynn Vivian Art Gallery and Museum, Alexandra Road. 10.30–5.30 (10.30–5.30). Tel: 0792 55006

LONDON GALLERIES

British Museum
Great Russell Street WC1B 3DG. 10–5 (2.30–6). Tel: 636 1555
Courtauld Institute Galleries
Somerset House, Strand, London, WC2R ORN. 10–5 (2–5). Tel: 873 2526
Dulwich Picture Gallery
College Road SE21. Tue–Sat 10–1; 2–5 (2–5). Closed Mondays. Tel: 693 5254
Iveagh Bequest, Kenwood
Hampstead Lane NW3. Apr–Sep 10–7 (10–7); Oct (10–5); Nov–Jan 10–4 (10–4); Feb–Mar 10–5 (10–5). Tel: 348 1286
Leighton House
12 Holland Park Road W14. 11–5. Mon–Sat. Closed public holidays. 11–6 Mon–Fri; 11–5. Sat during temporary exhibitions. Tel: 602 3316
William Morris Gallery
Lloyd Park, Forest Road E17 4PP. Tue–Sat 10–1, 2–5. Closed Mondays (1st Sun of the month 10–12, 2–5). Tel: 527 5544 ext. 4390
National Gallery
Trafalgar Square WC2N 5DN. 10–6 (2–6). Tel: 839 3321
(Publications 839 1912)
National Portrait Gallery
St Martin's Place WC2H 0HE. 10–5; Sat 10–6 (2–6). Tel: 930 1552
The Queen's Gallery
Buckingham Palace SW1. Tue–Sat 10.30–5 (2–5). Closed Mondays (except bank holidays). Tel: 930 4832
Tate Gallery
Millbank SW1P 4RG. 10–5.50 (2–5.50). Tel: 887 8000 (Publications 834 5651/2)
Victoria and Albert Museum
Cromwell Road SW7. Mon–Thur and Sat 10–5.50 (2.30–5.50). Closed Fridays. Tel: 589 6371 ext. 372
Wallace Collection
Manchester Square W1. 10–5 (2–5). Tel: 935 0687